ANOTHER VIETNAM

ANOTHER VIETNAM

PICTURES OF THE WAR FROM THE OTHER SIDE

TIM PAGE

EDITED BY

DOUG NIVEN AND CHRIS RILEY

FOREWORD BY

HENRY ALLEN

☐ NATIONAL GEOGRAPHIC

WASHINGTON, D.C.

Nam Ha Province, 1968

Villagers in the Thanh Liem district in this Northern coastal province say goodbye to young soldiers going to the front. Some of the recruits were too poor to afford shoes, but "men who were accepted into the army brought honor to their families," recalls the photographer, "and morale among the young recruits was high."

MAI NAM

Vinh Phu Province, September 4, 1966

A color greeting card distributed in 1967 shows an American F-105 fighter-bomber falling to Earth after being shot down in the Red River Delta region. The pilot drifts beneath his parachute at upper right. Capturing pilot and plummeting craft in a single frame was a rare feat, and this became a classic image in the North.

MAI NAM

Greeting from
VIETNAM

THE VOICE OF VIETNAM
56-58 QUAN SU STREET — HANOI

CONTENTS

Ngang Dua, 1960 Viet Cong guerrillas move through "fighting holes" in abandoned South Vietnamese houses. The holes were made by the Viet Minh during their struggle with the French in the early 1950s. Like the tunnel complexes dug by the Viet Minh, and later the Viet Cong, the fighting holes permitted insurgents to move through a village unseen.
LE CHAU

THE FACES OF FUTURES PAST

HENRY ALLEN

FOREWORD This book is about faces, really—the faces of the communist Vietnamese who drove France out of Vietnam, then killed Americans till we got the idea too, then destroyed the anti-communist Army of the Republic of Vietnam. And it's about how North Vietnamese photographers saw those faces, and showed them to their people.

You see heroes, tanks, trucks, burning American airplanes, and year after year after year of communist soldiers marching toward Saigon beneath shafted sunlight and the delicate heft of Asian landscape—many of these pictures are quite beautiful, well beyond the noble picturesque required by propaganda.

Mostly, though, you see faces, many of them posed for propaganda shots. There's a good deal of propaganda throughout the book, which is why there aren't a lot of pictures of downhearted, defeated, or dead Viet Cong, except for children massacred by the American war criminals. And there are a lot of pictures of The People cheering their young men off to war, The People pitching in to push trucks out of mud, The People rebuilding bridges with a determination that was their only weapon against the American bombs. And so many rifle-bearing militia women with faces like statues of Lenin—eyes lifted just above the horizon. And—of course—Jane Fonda, camp follower of the armies of the zeitgeist.

The trick, here, is to see beyond the propaganda of the pictures into a different culture, a different war. For example, no one is ever alone in these pictures—in contrast to our pictures of American soldiers, who so often seemed alone, even standing with their arms around their buddies' shoulders. Lone cowboys and alienation weren't cool among the communists, and irony doesn't skew their faces.

Anyway, we rarely saw Viet Cong the way you see them here. Sometimes we'd get a glimpse on a trail or in a tree line, or scrambling for cover under the flares that didn't light up the night as much as tear it apart with a trick of sucking all the color out of the world and converting it to incandescence.

Except in the sort of absurd encounter I had once, we only saw the faces of the Viet Cong when we killed them or took them prisoner. By then you couldn't see what their faces really looked like anymore. Dead faces looked dead, a universal quality of fly-specked anachronism. And the humiliated faces of prisoners—ours, theirs, anybody's, anytime—tend to remind you of sheep-killing dogs.

So we really didn't see them the way they looked, or the way they wanted their countrymen or commissars to see them—as examples of The New Man with faces focused on the inevitable victory promised by Marx; and as patriots repelling foreigners, which for thousands of years has been what it means to be Vietnamese. (I picked up a VC leaflet one day. It said in both English and Vietnamese: "When foreigners come there is war. When foreigners go, there is peace." I'd read some Vietnamese history and I couldn't argue.)

I'd imagined them looking sly but pathetic and stupid—either misguided nationalists or stooges of the communist slave masters. Once we did the old carrot-and-stick drill on them, they'd come over to where the Ford Fairlanes and the Princess telephones were, maybe even get a chance to demonstrate how to cut barbed wire on the *Ed Sullivan Show,* in the manner of Sam Snead hitting cotton golf balls into the audience.

This was in 1966. I was on a Marine civic action team along the coast, south of Da Nang, in Chu Lai, winning hearts and minds by giving away flour, cement, roofing tin, fishing engines, medical care, all the latest nation-building goodies. I had an easy time of it. Why would the Viet Cong want to kill the guys giving them the goodies?

Of course, they said they weren't Viet Cong, and they acted grateful in their preoccupied, measured, eye-averting way. In any case, a mind here and a heart there and pretty soon we'd win the war, even if come nightfall they kept springing up so far inside our perimeter that they could hit our water supply point with hand grenades, snap off some carbine fire, and then lie low while we fired back for hours at no one at all, at phantoms.

Then one day—it's an absurd story with the quality of a parable, like a lot of Vietnam stories—I got to stare at their real faces during a concert we organized in an outlying village.

Presenting: the Third Marine Division band under the noonday sun. Not much security—we still thought we should look like advisors, not troops, whenever possible. We didn't even wear flak jackets or helmets. Just American goodwill along with a hell of a solo on "Come Back to Sorrento" by a trumpeter who was putting out sweat like a dog shaking off pond water. The old women, old men, and children, filthy with paddy work, listened with anthropological curiosity. No young men in the crowd: They were off in the South Vietnamese Army or with the Viet Cong, or hiding from both.

About mid-concert, the Viet Cong showed up, five or six of them. Hard guys with faces set in a calm that showed they'd long ago traveled through insolence and contempt and kept right on going to a place I couldn't imagine. They were young, big and strong. They wore black pajamas that were clean, demonstrating that they weren't farmers. No weapons—they were too way cool for weapons. They were so very hip to the American hearts and minds routine. They had faces that said to me: "What are you going to do? Take your rifle off your shoulder and ruin the concert by shooting unarmed South Vietnamese?"

I said hello to them, the way I'd said hello to everyone else in the crowd. Something in their faces replied that I was being willfully ignorant, like all the Americans who still to this day believe they can make the whole world love them. They had faces as implacable as dentists' lamps. The message was: We know you know we know that you know now that we know something you'll leave Vietnam never knowing.

It was a show of force, really. And maybe, while they were at it, they picked out yet another one of our friendly village chiefs for beheading in the not-too-distant future. A tune or two later, they were gone, angels of ultimate hipness, waiting for sundown. I said to myself: "This is going to be a longer war than we thought."

It wasn't merely a question of their faces being Vietnamese. Our ARVN soldiers fighting for the South didn't look like this, at least where I was. They looked goofy and extraneous. Except for the blocky ones from the North, they had a fine-boned Malayan-stock thing about them that made their helmets and their sunglasses look too big. They worried a lot about sunglasses, cigarettes, and how they could get hold of a little Browning .25 for a pocket gun. I remember on one operation, we had to med-evac an ARVN officer because he had a stomachache.

As for the Americans, we had tight, tired faces from being scared all the time, but none of us seemed to be gazing at the future, VC style, because there wasn't any, beyond our personal rotation dates. Talk about alienation, and an army of time servers and individuals. No one talked about winning. It just didn't come up. The staff sergeants would say: "It ain't much of a war but it's the only war we got."

You didn't see faces chockful of intention, or eyes gazing at sublime inevitabilities in the manner of the North Vietnamese faces in this book. A news magazine said my outfit had landed "lean, hungry and looking for a fight." That got quite a laugh.

It was a great war for the media, though, way greater than it was for the people who fought it. Name anybody CBS's Walter Cronkite covered who was as important as Walter Cronkite. Less famous than Cronkite, but way cooler were the freelance photographers. Such vagabond authenticity, such marginalized romance: Sean Flynn, Tim Page, Dana Stone—in the war but not of it, the secret heroes of their own pictures. They and countless others didn't shoot pictures of warriors, like the North Vietnamese, they shot pictures of war.

Big difference.

Our photography showed the horror, destruction, fatigue, and haunted eyes with no visions of historical inevitability in them. There were pictures of dead civilians, burned children, the shooting of prisoners, the dragging of bodies behind tanks, and American faces resigned but persevering, like masks in an existential allegory. Soldiers cowered and crouched, suffered through the hateful swamps. They cried and died. They got high. Their pride came out looking like sadistic mania, and their bravery was either pathos or stupidity. Their morale showed itself as "feelings," which are no morale at all.

This was high drama for the Age of Irony. It was supposed to be realism, but it was propaganda, too, furthering the cause of "truth," which seemed to be a combination of nihilism, pity, and self-righteousness entitling all its beholders and believers to feel a little superior to something, I'm not sure what.

Maybe all news about wars is propaganda, one way or the other. It's so easy to keep doing it that way. The propaganda changes the way faces look and the way photographers want to shoot them.

I look at this book and I sense the remnants of me as a little boy looking at photographs of my father's war, when the men looked brave and just. Look at the cover picture: Three Viet Cong charging across the rubble at Quang Tri, not an ambiguity in sight, big bravery in the broad daylight. The little boy voice in me says: Yes! That's the kind of war I want to fight in when I grow up.

NEXT PAGE: THE VOLUNTEER YOUTH, mostly female, fill in bomb craters, rebuilding. We would have shown the destruction of the bodies in them. Then recruits waving back to a waving crowd seeing them off to the war. Look at the art and beauty of a file of soldiers moving through holes in inside walls that connected one building to the next, a telescope made of rubble and the soldiers moving through it.

Here's a beautiful girl with a rifle, a conical hat, and eyes looking over her shoulder, that Lenin-vision look again. Now two Viet Cong planting American Claymore mines in the Mekong Delta in 1973: What leg-muscled, headbanded sculpture this is, thighs echoing the angles of rifles, faces serious the way adults are serious—adult seriousness having passed out of fashion in America, where youth worshiped its own youth, and found it to be a moral virtue.

An old man strides through rubble with his staff in one hand. Women pull fishing nets in the cozy perfection of a composition built on circles and diagonals. A stoop-shouldered Viet Cong prisoner stands in front of a Peoples' court. Five Viet Cong pose in a tableau of jungle and machine guns in the sunlight. The People wait with ideal patience for fish sauce to be ladled into containers, all cooperating for the benefit of all. And my God, even the combat pictures look optimistic, with soldiers charging and shooting in orgies of courage and self-sacrifice.

Well, yes, propaganda. But they believed it, the people who made it and the people who saw it. The same way so many Americans believed the pictures they saw in *Life* magazine.

These are pictures by and of people who were fighting for victory. Ours are pictures of people fighting for a just settlement of political issues. It's easier to fight for victory, I suspect. Too bad they've done so little with that victory.

I returned to Vietnam in 1999. It's a country of many charms and a great many corruptions. Maybe they're not very good at peace. Their noble, implacable, Leninist faces were gone. I almost missed them.

Nam Ha Province, September 1972 Vietnamese journalists and foreign correspondents friendly to the North interview a wounded victim following the American bombing of the Thong Nhat health clinic. Such photographs were widely displayed in the North to demonstrate the impact on the civilian population of the U.S. bombing campaign.

LAM HONG

THROUGH THE PAST, SOFTLY

DOUG NIVEN

INTRODUCTION Somehow, an entire chapter has gone missing from the Vietnam War for those of us in the West. The mosaic that made up our collective memory of the war featured the same iconic images over and over—the curbside execution of a Viet Cong sapper; a monk committing self-immolation in a Saigon intersection; an American tank dragging the body of a Viet Cong soldier; the young girl burned by napalm and running down a road. And, finally, the helicopter about to lift off from a rooftop across from the American Embassy in Saigon, desperate humans waiting to get aboard. But that was our mosaic, a Western one. What photographs created the mosaic in the Vietnamese mind? Surely, the victors had their own set of images etched in the collective memory.

I first discovered images of the Vietnam War as a kid, poring over books at the local library. Those photographs, together with the many 1980s and '90s Hollywood films inspired by the war, painted my lasting visual backdrop of that conflict. As an aspiring photojournalist, I marveled at the images, most of them in black and white, of war photographers like Larry Burrows, Philip Jones Griffiths, and Don McCullin. They were my heroes,

DINH DANG DINH

Dinh Dang Dinh was Ho Chi Minh's personal photographer. Born in 1920 to a poor peasant family from Bac Ninh, Dinh became a young revolutionary in 1936, took up photography in 1941 in the resistance, and made his first photo of Uncle Ho in 1941. He took iconic photos of Ho until Ho's death in 1969, and Dinh's photos are still seen throughout Vietnam, having been made into stamps, postcards, and murals. Dinh founded the Vietnam Artistic Photographer's Association, which survives as Vietnam's largest association of photographers.

and written accounts of the Vietnam experience by Tim Page and Robert Sam Anson captured my imagination.

Yet, on the rare moments when I came across a photo from the "other side," shot by a Vietnamese photographer, the pictures always seemed faded, bleached and tiny, rarely larger than a postage stamp. They usually seemed added to a history book almost as an afterthought. As often as not, they showed some variation of an American POW being led away at gunpoint by a Vietnamese woman half his size.

It struck me as strange that not even a rudimentary picture of the enemy—aside from the cliché of the guerrilla in black pajamas—was represented in our collective mind's eye. The North Vietnamese soldiers and Viet Cong guerrillas couldn't have looked and acted that differently, I thought, from their South Vietnamese brethren. But a clear picture of them was missing. This mighty enemy never had a face.

THE VIETNAMESE have a long, rich tradition of arts and literature, so I was sure that a fraternity of former war photographers existed in Vietnam, unknown to us in the West. I imagined their photographs piled high in dusty offices in Hanoi, just waiting to be seen. After working as a news photographer myself in Phnom Penh, Cambodia, in the early '90s, I decided that I would try to find those photographers, collect their pictures and record their stories, with the simple goal of adding their images to our memory of the Vietnam War.

I quickly discovered that Vietnamese war photographers were similar to their Western/American counterparts in many ways. They were a warm, jovial group of retired men (no females had been Vietnamese war photographers), passionate about their life's work. Nearly all of them were still making photographs, though they were well into their 60s, 70s, and 80s. Their modest houses and tiny apartments in government housing projects were often lined with black-and-white photographs—none of them from the war. Instead, they reflected classic Asian themes: Wispy bamboo towering over rice fields; pretty girls dressed in the traditional Vietnamese *ao dai;* faces from the many ethnic hill tribes.

As I sat in their living rooms with them, drinking bitter tea or homemade brandy, their life stories began to unfold. They had struggled with many of the same challenges as their Western counterparts. They had argued with their editors about subject matter and journalistic principles; complained about having to work with fickle writers; and, just like us, snipped the best frames from their rolls to keep for themselves, knowing that some less capable or less caring person down the line would be handling their film.

Like all photographers, they spoke in fond detail of their cameras, specifically which models could survive mud, heat, and humidity best. They typically owned only one lens, a standard 50mm. A few of them had huge, heavy Kodak press cameras made in the 1940s, not exactly practical for war photography. They were the same kind of hulking camera that Weegee used to record his famous street scenes of New York City in the '40s. Weegee had carried his camera equipment around in his car. The Vietnamese photographers didn't have cars, but they managed to lug those cameras around anyway. And the payoff was worth it: The bulky cameras produced large, rich negatives, brimming with information.

No matter what size camera they used, all of the Vietnamese war photographers had had to plan each shot carefully, so as not to waste precious film. Even in the heat of battle, every shot had to count. Motor drives were not part of their equipment, and none of them had the luxury of simply loading and shooting another roll of film. In fact, one photographer, who was also a writer, used only one roll of film for the duration of the war. He didn't know how to change film, and in any case he didn't have a second roll.

DOAN CONG TINH

Doan Cong Tinh, born in 1943 to an army family in Hanoi, was nick-named "King of the Battlefield" by his colleagues. Tinh worked as an army photographer, carrying both a camera and an AK-47, and took enor-mous risks to make photographs dur-ing key battles, standing up while his fellow soldiers hunkered down. His frontline images were so valuable and unique he was encouraged to retire in 1973, two years before the war ended. Tinh married an army doctor and currently lobbies for war veterans.

Processing chemicals were mixed in tea saucers, with water from mountain streams. Exposed film was developed late at night, under the stars, when other colleagues were sleeping, somewhere in a liberated zone or along the Truong Son, the mountain range through Vietnam that we called the Ho Chi Minh Trail. They often processed only half a roll of film at a time, so that, in case of an accident, the whole roll wouldn't be ruined. They told me they had the largest darkroom in the world, the night sky their only safelight.

All of the photographers I met harbored poignant memories of the Truong Son. As dangerous and arduous as it was, it inspired some of Vietnam's best folklore, art, and songs. The photographers were told by their superiors not to take photo-graphs of the trail, yet upon seeing it, they couldn't resist and sneaked shots.

After a photographer and I had shared our first few cups of tea, the scrap-books, diaries, bags, and boxes of photographs would be brought out. At that point, the photographer's wife would slip quietly away into a back room, as if something secret were about to take place. Strangely enough, the photo prints of the war that came out of those scrapbooks and boxes were small and faded, just like the images I had seen reproduced occasionally in books. Sadly, in the many years since the war ended, the Vietnamese photographers had never had enough photographic paper to print their images any larger or better. It seemed wrong to me that their work had not been seen, wasn't known. And strange that no one had come knocking on their doors, asking about their work before me.

One photographer I met, Doan Cong Tinh, whose images are some of the most powerful from the war, kept his film under the bathroom sink. Vo Anh Khanh still keeps his negatives in a U.S. ammunition case, with a bed of roasted Vietnamese rice for a desiccant. His negatives look like they were made yesterday. Another photographer presented his life's work in plastic bags brim-ming with dusty negatives, nearly all of them never before printed.

They let me take their negatives away for processing, and it was thrilling to see the powerful images rise up from the scratched negatives and dog-eared prints I had seen on their tables. I hoped these images would replace the faded and yellowing prints the photographers themselves had preserved so carefully. It was exciting to see how their photographs began to fill a void, painting a more complete picture of the war. With those negatives and fading prints, I knew that, given time and abundant amounts of photographic paper and chemicals, we could bring their images and their experiences back to life.

After mixing hundreds of gallons of photo chemicals on hotel balconies and washing prints in hotel bathtubs, I finally finished the printing. I met with each photographer to return his film and show him the images I had made from his negatives. For some of them, seeing their photographs printed large for the first time brought tears to their eyes. Experiences like that were what helped me finish the project and remain some of my most cherished memories from Vietnam.

After one particularly long session of printing vintage photographs in Saigon, I headed to Hanoi to show a photography director at the Vietnam News Agency his southern counterparts' work. Really, I didn't have much to discuss with him, but the box of prints on my lap caught his attention. This bureaucrat reveled in his unknown colleagues' work, and he immediately agreed to join my project. Many photographers told me, too, that this project was something they had wanted to do themselves.

Yet, surprisingly, of those I spoke to, many didn't know of each other and had never seen each other's work. Often, this was due to Vietnam's impressive geography—long, thin, and mountainous. But in other cases, it was probably because the photographers wanted to put the war years behind them and move on with their lives.

Among the ones who did know each other, a sometimes not-so-friendly

NGUYEN DINH UU

Nguyen Dinh Uu, born in 1918, was also an army photographer, though he was affiliated with *Viet-Nam Pictorial* magazine, which was distributed internationally. Uu was a teacher to many of the war's photographers, and began taking pictures in 1947 of French POWs. Uu rode his bicycle to the front lines in both the French and American conflicts, once travelling more than 300 miles from Hanoi to the Demilitarized Zone (DMZ), dodging bomb craters and waiting for lulls in the fighting to move on.

VO ANH KHANH

Vo Anh Khanh, born in 1939, was the Mekong Delta photographer. Khanh began photography in 1957 with a family-owned photo shop, which had to be abandoned when the war came to their small town of Bac Lieu. Khanh joined the revolution in 1961 and worked with the National Liberation Front, though he spent most of the war working alone, and despite several attempts to send his photographs north, none of his photos ever made it to Hanoi. Khanh lugged a large press camera around and hid his negatives in buried ammunition boxes, using roasted rice to act as a desiccant.

competition could mean that one photographer did not want to introduce me to his best friend—also a photographer, with better pictures. On the other extreme, Asian standards of modesty sometimes complicated things. I had to track down many photographers myself, even though they were aware from their friends that I was searching for them.

Sadly, many of the photographers' names will never be known, because the images came from Vietnamese agencies and photo archives, which varied from excellent to terrible. Fortunately, the Vietnam News Agency protected its film archives in cool, low humidity conditions, so their material was in good shape. But many of their negatives, and those of various other news agencies and newspapers in Hanoi and in the liberated zones along the Vietnam-Cambodia border, had been sent without proper captions or the names of the photographers. A lot of photographers had used a nom de guerre, their identities never revealed to anyone. The photographers I talked to said that most of their colleagues sent in film under false names to protect themselves. If their film had been discovered by the enemy and their identity known, they could have been executed. But they had another reason as well. They felt that they were part of a much larger struggle, and their names were somehow unimportant. They remain to this day unidentified.

For the same reasons, the content and location of a photograph often had to be disguised. This was frustrating in my work—information being vitally important to me as a photojournalist. But so many years after the war, when so many of the people involved in it had faded into the shadows, I sometimes had to be content with just the image itself, no matter what it was of or who had made it.

Vietnamese war photography as a whole was not directed from one single place, so huge chunks are missing in the chronology of the conflict. Frequently, photographers were not allowed to the front lines, as death there was too often unavoidable. Because there were so few of them and their skills so highly valued as witnesses of history, the photographers were often prohibited by orders from going where they wanted. Tragically, all of the Viet Cong photographers who documented the Tet offensive of 1968, aside from Lam Tan Tai, died covering it, and Tai himself lost an eye, as well as his film and camera. During the Easter offensive in 1972, the photographers were unleashed en masse along the DMZ, though even then the Quang Tri citadel was off-limits. Only photographer Doan Cong Tinh made it there, disobeying direct orders and risking his career—and life—to get shots inside the citadel.

VIETNAM'S WAR PHOTOGRAPHERS came from many different backgrounds. Vo Anh Khanh lived in the southernmost tip of the country, the Ca Mau Peninsula. He ran the family photo business until 1960, when the first waves of the war came to his small town. The war forced him to close his shop. To Khanh, 21 years old at the time, it was only natural to sacrifice the family business and join the war effort. Khanh hauled around a heavy Kodak press camera. It was all he had.

Nguyen Duy Kien was a young aristocrat in the 1930s, a time when only wealthy Vietnamese could afford to own cameras. Kien had been happy making photos of beauty contests and landscapes, until, in 1946, French expeditionary forces razed a neighborhood near his home. Witnessing such a scene, Kien felt compelled to record it for history. His 80-year-old widow still proudly shows his work to interested parties, the images propped up in a corner of their once grand Hanoi mansion. Now, she shares the house—nationalized in the 1950s and divided into apartments—with strangers.

Uncle Ho's personal photographer, Dinh Dang Dinh, fell into the profession while hiding out with Ho in the Viet Bac, the Vietnamese hinterland, in the 1940s. Ho himself had had a job retouching photographs while living in Paris in the 1920s, and he encouraged Dinh with his famous mantra, "Obstacles make you

DUONG THANH PHONG
Duong Thanh Phong, born in 1940, was the Cu Chi tunnel photographer, having been born into a revolutionary family along the Cambodian border. Phong began working as a darkroom technician during the French conflict and soon became an expert at making fake identification cards for the Viet Minh guerrillas. He worked clandestinely in a government-controlled village until 1965, when he was forced to flee to the liberated zones.

MAI NAM

Mai Nam, born in 1931, made some of the most memorable photos of daily life during the war. Nam worked for the *Hanoi Tien Phong (Pioneer)* newspaper his entire career, and with a few exceptions, stayed away from the front lines, striving to record the efforts and courage of ordinary Vietnamese affected by the war north of the DMZ. Famous for his photo of an American plane tumbling to Earth, its pilot floating down in a parachute, Mai Nam now makes home-made brandy and photographs beauty pageants.

clever." While in the Viet Bac, Dinh processed his film in homemade bamboo trays lined with beeswax he gathered himself; he washed the film in mountain streams. The black-and-white negatives produced during that period look like they were exposed and processed yesterday, his techniques were so flawless, his materials so durable.

Individual photographers tended to specialize in particular themes, often reflecting the focus of their newspapers or magazines. Mai Nam concentrated on young people and daily life. Doan Cong Tinh was the photographer for the Vietnam People's Army and gained the nickname "king of the battlefield." Having served as a Viet Minh soldier fighting the French in 1949, Le Minh Truong traveled throughout Vietnam, Laos, and Cambodia on foot, always searching for beauty amid the chaos and destruction. Van Bao described his own photographic style as "socialist realism," and many of his images were reproduced internationally. Dinh Dang Dinh was given a six-month assignment to cover the swarming activity of transport battalions and troop movements along the Ho Chi Minh Trail; he lost all of his equipment and a hundred rolls of film in a bombing raid in 1974. Dinh says he still wakes up at night in a sweat, still devastated by the loss of this film.

Almost to a man, the Vietnamese photographers were self-taught. Even today, no school exists in Vietnam to teach photography. Some of the war photographers had seen photo exhibitions at the French Information Service during the colonial regime, then had scraped together enough money to buy their first photography book.

Recipes for photochemistry were copied from books at the library or passed among friends, the ingredients mixed from scratch. Film came from Germany, China, Japan, and Czechoslovakia and was always in tight supply. Magazines from Europe, America, and Japan were bought at local bookshops. Some found themselves drawn to the patriotic images from Stalin's Russia or Mao's China. The bold, graphic style of these images could be copied easily in Vietnam, where the themes of revolution and struggle struck a chord.

A few photographers have now had their own books of war photography published in Vietnam, but curiously I couldn't find them for sale in local shops. This, I concluded, was because the Vietnamese government is still struggling to arrive at an "official" version of the war. Maybe we in America are struggling with the same issue. The photographers were also expected to self-finance publications of their works, an impossibility for most of them. So their photographs have remained hidden in archives, under sinks, in closets, instead of being seen. Until now.

THE RESOUNDING THEME from all the photographers I spoke to was that the war years were the best of their lives. They had realized their dreams and ambitions as photographers; they cherished their memories of sharing sweet potatoes and tobacco with colleagues in the central highlands; they even missed the meager meals of boiled rice and vegetables gathered in the forest and cooked in rough bivouacs along the Ho Chi Minh Trail. Food just tasted better back then, they said. The hardships they shared bred a kind of camaraderie and love that they insisted they had not experienced since. Their bonds with the people, the soldiers, and the fellow journalists were unshakable.

At one point I asked each of them if they actually missed the war years, despite the dangers and hardships. Their answers were all the same, usually given with some embarrassment. They all said that since the war had ended, their lives had become pedestrian, routine, lacking in meaning. The wrinkles on their faces seemed to disappear as they talked of the war years. Yes, they missed their war greatly—but they were glad it was over.

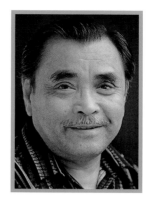

LAM TAN TAI

Lam Tan Tai, a southerner born in 1935, was a revolutionary student who studied in both Hanoi and Moscow. Tai returned to Vietnam from Russia and was sent down the Ho Chi Minh Trail to the liberated zone at Tay Ninh, where he was assigned to set up the Liberation News Agency in the malaria-infested jungle. During the Tet offensive, Tai entered Saigon with his Viet Cong reporter colleagues, who were all killed. Alone, and blinded in one eye during the famous battle near the Saigon TV tower, Tai escaped back to the jungle where he continued to coordinate coverage of the National Liberation Front from the jungle. He died in 2001.

CHINA

Tropic of Cancer

Ho Giang
CAO BANG
Cao Bang
HA GIANG
Nui Con Voi
LAO CAI
Lao Cai
Black (Da) Red (Hong)
LAI CHAU
Fan Si Pan
BAC
LANG
SON
TUYEN
QUANG
Lang Son
YEN BAI
THAI
NGHIA
LO
VINH
PHU
Viet
Bac
Thai Nguyen
Dien Bien Phu
(Dien Bien)
Phu Tho
Viet Tri
Dac
Giang
HA BAC
QUANG NINH
Luc Ngan
SON LA
Son Tay
HANOI
Ha Dong
HAI
Hai Duong
Dao Cai Bau
Hong Gai
Fai Tsi Long
Cam Pha
Archipelago
HOA
BINH
HA
TAY
KIEN AN
HAIPHONG
Nam
Dinh
THAI BINH
NINH
BINH
NAM
HA
Thai Binh
Ninh Binh
Red River
Delta

NORTH

Thanh Hoa

Gulf of Tonkin

THANH HOA

Hieu

Hon Me

VIETNAM

NGHE AN

Con

Vinh

HA TINH

Ha Tinh

LEGEND

⊛ National capital
• Other city
— International boundary
— Provincial boundary
····· Demilitarized zone
→ Trail
⤨ Pass

Map boundaries and names reflect conditions in 1975; present-day names appear in parentheses.

QUANG BINH
Mu Gia Pass
Dong Hoi
Ben Karai Pass
Vinh Linh
DEMILITARIZED ZONE
(Demarcation Line, July 22, 1954)
17th Parallel
Gio Linh
Dong Ha
Tchepone
(Xépôn)
Con Thien
Quang Tri
QUANG TRI
Khe Sanh
Hue
THUA THIEN
Da Nang Bay
(Vung Da Nang)
Da Nang
DA NANG
QUANG NAM
Cu Lao Cham
Hoi An

INDOCHINA

CHINA

BURMA
NORTH
Hanoi ⊛
Gulf of Tonkin
VIETNAM
Hainan
LAOS
Vientiane ⊛
THAILAND
SOUTH
Bangkok ⊛
VIETNAM
CAMBODIA
Phnom Penh ⊛
Saigon ⊛
Gulf of Thailand
South China Sea

Saravan
(Salavan)
Tam Ky
Chu Lai
Cu Lao Re
QUANG TIN
My Lai
QUANG
NGAI
Quang Ngai
Attapu
KONTUM
Kontum
(Kon Tum)
HO CHI MINH TRAIL
PLEIKU
Pleiku
(Play Ku)
BINH
DINH
Qui Nhon

SOUTH

CENTRAL
Hau Bon
(Cheo Reo)
PHU
YEN
Vung Xuan Dai
PHU BON
Tuy Hoa
Da Rang
DARLAC
HIGHLANDS
Ban Me Thuot
(Buon Me Thuot)
KHANH
HOA
Hon Lon
Vung Van Phong
Nha Trang
Hon Tre

VIETNAM

QUANG DUC
TUYEN DUC
CAM RANH
Cam Ranh
Cam Ranh Bay
(Vung Cam Ranh)
NINH
THUAN
Da Lat
LAM DONG
Phan Rang
Bao Loc

Kratie
CAMBODIA
Phuoc Binh
(Ba Ra)
Loc Ninh
BINH
LONG
An Loc
(Han Quan)
TAY NINH
PHUOC
LONG
LONG
KHANH
BINH
TUY
SIHANOUK TRAIL
PHNOM
PENH ⊛
Tay Ninh
BINH
DUONG
Bien Hoa
Xuan Loc
BINH THUAN
Phan Thiet
Trang Bang
HAU
NGHIA
Cu Chi
BIEN
HOA
Sihanoukville
(Kompong Som)
Chau Phu
CHAU
DOC
KIEN
PHONG
KIEN TUONG
Plain of Reeds
LONG
AN
SAIGON
(Ho Chi Minh City)
Tan An
PHUOC TUY
Ham Tan
VUNG TAU
AN
GIANG
Ha Tien
Long Xuyen
Sa Dec
DINH
TUONG
GO CONG
Vung Tau
Dao Phu Quoc
KIEN GIANG
Rach Gia
VINH
LONG
Can Tho
Vinh Long
Go Cong
Truc Giang
(Ben Tre)
KIEN HOA
Rach Gia Bay
(Vung Rach Gia)
PHONG
DINH
Phu Vinh
(Tra Vinh)
VINH
BINH
Mekong
River Delta
U Minh
Forest
CHUONG
THIEN
Soc Trang
BA XUYEN
Bac Lieu
Quan Long (Ca Mau)
BAC
LIEU
AN XUYEN
Con Son
Ca Mau
Peninsula
Coa Song Bay Hap
Hon Khoai

SCALE

0 — Kilometers — 100
0 — Statute Miles — 100

1951: Viet Minh during the Tran Hung Dao campaign against the French

1954

May 7: Vietnamese forces occupy the French command post at **Dien Bien Phu,** and the French commander orders his troops to cease fire. The battle had lasted 55 days.

1959

A specialized North Vietnamese Army unit, Group 559, is formed to create a supply route from North Vietnam to Viet Cong forces in South Vietnam. With the approval of Prince Sihanouk of Cambodia, Group 559 develops a primitive route along the Vietnamese-Cambodian border, with offshoots into Vietnam along its entire length. This eventually becomes known as the **Ho Chi Minh Trail.**

1961

President John F. Kennedy orders more help for the South Vietnamese government in its war against the Viet Cong guerrillas.

December 11: American helicopters arrive at docks in South Vietnam along with 400 U.S. personnel, who will fly and maintain the aircraft.

1962

January 12: In Operation Chopper, helicopters flown by U.S. Army pilots ferry 1,000 South Vietnamese soldiers to sweep an NLF stronghold near Saigon. It marks America's first combat missions against the Viet Cong.

1963

January 2: At the hamlet of Ap Bac, the Viet Cong 514th Battalion and local guerrilla forces ambush the South Vietnamese Army's 7th division. For the first time, the Viet Cong stand their ground against American machinery and South Vietnamese soldiers. Almost 400 South Vietnamese are killed or wounded. Three American advisors are slain.

1965: Operation Rolling Thunder, bombing the North

1969: U.S. combat deaths in Vietnam exceed 33,629

1972: Napalm dropped by mistake on village

1975: Evacuation of Saigon

1964

August 4: The captain of the U.S.S. Maddox reports that his vessel has been fired on and that an attack is imminent. Though he later says that no attack took place, six hours after the initial report a retaliation against North Vietnam is ordered by President Johnson. American jets bomb two naval bases and destroy a major oil facility. Two U.S. planes are downed in the attack.

August 7: The U.S. Congress passes the **Gulf of Tonkin Resolution,** giving President Johnson the power to take whatever actions he sees necessary to defend Southeast Asia.

November 1: Two days before the U.S. presidential election, Viet Cong mortars shell Bien Hoa Air Base near Saigon. Four Americans are killed, 76 wounded. Five B-57 bombers are destroyed, and 15 are damaged.

1965

February 7: A U.S. helicopter base and advisory compound in the central highlands of South Vietnam are attacked by NLF commandos. Nine Americans are killed and more than 70 are wounded. President Johnson immediately orders U.S. Navy fighter-bombers to attack military targets just inside North Vietnam.

February 13: President Johnson authorizes Operation Rolling Thunder, a limited but long-lasting bombing offensive. Its aim is to force North Vietnam to stop supporting Viet Cong guerrillas in the South.

April 7: The U.S. offers North Vietnam economic aid in exchange for peace, but the offer is summarily rejected. Two weeks later, President Johnson raises America's combat strength in Vietnam to more than 60,000 troops.

November 17: Elements of the 66th North Vietnamese Regiment moving east toward Plei Mei encounter and ambush an American battalion. When fighting ends that night, 60 percent of the Americans are casualties, and almost one of every three soldiers in the battalion have been killed.

1966

January 8: U.S. forces launch Operation Crimp to capture the Viet Cong's headquarters for the Saigon area, which is believed to be located in the district of **Cu Chi.** Though the area in Cu Chi is razed and repeatedly patrolled, American forces fail to locate any significant Viet Cong base.

December: American forces in Vietnam reach 385,000 men, plus an additional 60,000 sailors stationed offshore. More than 6,000 Americans have been killed in this year, and 30,000 have been wounded. In comparison, an estimated 61,000 Viet Cong have been killed. NVA troops, however, now number over 280,000.

1967

January-May: Two North Vietnamese divisions, operating out of the DMZ that separates North and South Vietnam, launch heavy bombardments of American bases south of the DMZ. These bases include **Khe Sanh, the Rockpile, Cam Lo, Dong Ha, Con Thien,** and **Gio Linh**.

January 8: American forces begin Operation Cedar Falls, which is intended to drive Viet Cong forces from the Iron Triangle, a 60-square mile area lying between the Saigon River and Route 13. Nearly 16,000 American troops and 14,000 soldiers of the South Vietnamese Army move into the Iron Triangle, but they encounter no major resistance. Huge quantities of enemy supplies are captured. Over 19 days, 72 Americans are killed, victims mostly of booby traps and snipers emerging from concealed tunnels. Seven hundred and twenty Viet Cong are killed.

May: Desperate air battles rage in the skies over Hanoi and Haiphong. American air forces shoot down 26 North Vietnamese jets, decreasing the North's pilot strength by half.

1968

January 21: At 5:30 a.m., a shattering barrage of shells, mortars, and rockets slams into the Marine base at **Khe Sanh**. Eighteen Marines are killed instantly, 40 are wounded. The initial attack continues for two days.

January 30: On the **Tet** holiday, Viet Cong units surge into action over the length and breadth of South Vietnam. In more than 100 cities and towns, shock attacks by Viet Cong sapper-commandos are followed by wave after wave of supporting troops. By the end of the city battles, 37,000 Viet Cong troops deployed for Tet have been killed. Many more have been wounded or captured, and the fighting had created more than a half million civilian refugees.

February 23: Over 1,300 artillery rounds hit the Marine base at **Khe Sanh** and its outposts, more than on any previous day of attacks. To withstand the constant assaults, bunkers are rebuilt to withstand 82-mm mortar rounds.

March 16: In the hamlet of My Lai, U.S. Charlie Company kills about 200 civilians. Although only one member of the division is tried and found guilty of war crimes, the repercussions of the atrocity are felt throughout the Army.

April 8: U.S. forces in Operation Pegasus finally retake Route 9, ending the siege of Khe Sanh. A 77-day battle, Khe Sanh had been the biggest single battle of the Vietnam War to that point.

November 1: After three and a half years, **Operation Rolling Thunder** comes to an end. In total, the campaign had cost more than 900 American aircraft. Eight hundred and eighteen pilots are dead or missing, and hundreds are in captivity. Nearly 120 Vietnamese planes have been destroyed in air combat or accidents, or by friendly fire. According to U.S. estimates, 182,000 North Vietnamese civilians have been killed.

1969

January: President Richard M. Nixon promises to achieve "Peace With Honor." His aim is to negotiate a settlement that will allow the half million U.S. troops in Vietnam to be withdrawn, while still allowing South Vietnam to survive.

February 22: In a major offensive, assault teams and artillery attack American bases all over South Vietnam, killing 1,140 Americans.

June 8: President Nixon meets with South Vietnamese President Nguyen Van Thieu on Midway Island in the Pacific, and he announces that 25,000 U.S. troops will be withdrawn immediately.

1971

While herbicides containing Dioxin were banned for use by the U.S. Department of Agriculture in 1968, spraying of Agent Orange continues in Vietnam until 1971. Operation Ranchhand has sprayed 11 million gallons of Agent Orange—containing 240 pounds of the lethal chemical Dioxin—on South Vietnam. More than one-seventh of the country's total area has been laid waste.

1972

January 1: Only 133,000 U.S. servicemen remain in South Vietnam. Two thirds of America's troops have gone in two years. The ground war is now almost exclusively the responsibility of South Vietnam, which has over 1,000,000 men enlisted in its armed forces.

April 27: North Vietnamese forces again battle toward **Quang Tri city**. The defending South Vietnamese division retreats. By April 29, the NVA takes Dong Ha, and by May 1, Quang Tri City.

December 18: By order of the president, a new bombing campaign starts against the North Vietnamese. Operation Linebacker Two lasts for 12 days, including a three-day bombing period by up to 120 B-52s.

1973

January 27: All warring parties in the Vietnam War sign a cease-fire.

March: The last American combat soldiers leave South Vietnam, though military advisors and Marines, who are protecting U.S. installations, remain. For the United States, the war is officially over. Of the more than 3 million Americans who have served in the war, almost 58,000 are dead, and over 1,000 are missing in action. Some 150,000 Americans were seriously wounded.

1974

January: Though they are still too weak to launch a full-scale offensive, the North Vietnamese have rebuilt their divisions in the South and have captured key areas.

1975

January 6: In a disastrous loss for the South Vietnamese, the NVA take Phuoc Long city and the surrounding province. The attack, a blatant violation of the Paris peace agreement, produces no retaliation from the United States.

April: Five weeks into its campaign, the North Vietnamese Army has made stunning gains. Twelve provinces and more than eight million people are under its control. The South Vietnamese Army has lost its best units, over a third of its men, and almost half its weapons.

April 30: At 4:03 a.m., two U.S. Marines are killed in a rocket attack at Saigon's Tan Son Nhut airport. They are the last Americans to die in the Vietnam War. At dawn, the last Marines of the force guarding the U.S. embassy lift off. Only hours later, looters ransack the embassy, and North Vietnamese tanks roll into Saigon, ending the war. In 15 years, nearly a million NVA and Viet Cong troops and a quarter of a million South Vietnamese soldiers have died. Hundreds of thousands of civilians have been killed.

WANING DAYS OF
FRENCH INDOCHINA

CHAPTER ONE This is a tome of resurrection, the resurrection not just of photographic images but of the photographers who made them. It is the unveiling of a perspective on a period of shared history, a point of view that we in the West had not really understood. We had not been aware, even those of us in the Western media, of the amount of material photographed by the Vietnamese—by the dedicated Communist Party members in the North and by the National Liberation Front in the South. The work of some of the Northern photographers saw a modicum of exposure to the world of print, the efforts of those in the South were hidden in shadow—until now. An enormous Pandora's box, their work is a trove of images only marginally explored or exploited, images we would likely consider iconic or Pulitzer candidates.

Over a decade ago, on one of my first trawls through Hanoi's photographic archives, I was looking for the works of Vietnamese photographers on the communist side who had perished during the long years of conflict, from 1945 to 1975. I was astounded by the breadth and styles of the war photography I discovered. The staffs of the Vietnam News Agency

Dien Bien Phu, 1954

A French supply plane goes down in the climactic battle of the Indochina War. The French garrison at Dien Bien Phu relied on air resupply, but Viet Minh artillery succeeded in downing numerous planes. By the time the communists overran the outpost, 2,293 of its 12,000 defenders had been killed, including two American advisors.

PHOTOGRAPHER UNKNOWN

Viet-Nam Pictorial, 1972
The monthly magazine that show-
cased the work of Northern war
photographers for foreign audiences
occasionally featured artwork, such
as this painting of fighting in Laos
by artist/photographer The Dinh.

(VNA) and later the Vietnam Artistic Photographers Association (VAPA) gradually joined in my search, helping me uncover a wealth of imagery. Ultimately, we uncovered more than buried photographs.

Over the course of our investigations, the panoply of recent Vietnamese history—the revolution, the nation's liberation, then reunification—was replayed. We were unearthing images still uncomfortable to both former warring sides. Initially, on my first foray, I had come home with more than 120 images taken by Vietnamese photographers lost in action to place beside those of the 73 Western photographers who had been killed over the 30 years of conflict. From this, *Requiem* was born, the book to appease and honor the spirits of our fallen comrades—a tribute to the era when photojournalism still had an impact on world consciousness.

The Vietnamese photographer The Dinh, in some ways a metaphor for the current book, serves as a perfect example of resurrection. Once on the official rolls of the dead, he is now back among the living. Having heard of his own demise, reported in the book *Requiem* and in a documentary on Vietnam television, he wrote to the director of VAPA, lamenting the untimely appearance of his obituary. From KIA to MIA to very much alive, a symbol in himself of modern Vietnamese history.

Like much Vietnamese photography, many of the images that I found in my searches were only copy negatives, the originals long ago eroded, corroded, or destroyed by time and war. What survives has been preserved with diligence and loving care against the assaults of a climate that breeds fungus on every surface, that eats photographic prints into moldy piles and makes negatives look like they've been melted in a projector.

The images we found in our search were usually provided at 60 cents for a 5x7 print of questionable quality. The one 8x10 that I purchased cost 90 cents; its photographer had defied certain party edicts followed by his Northern comrades not to photograph themselves or the dead. But this defiant image verged on the surreal—the photographer's shadow cast over a crater littered with the debris of war, including the burned cadaver of a Southern soldier.

At the time of that first research, I hadn't focused on frames taken by photographers who were still alive. But the images were indelible, a collection filed in the back of the mind. A cache waiting to be opened.

The light that finally illumined those shadowy repositories of history was turned on by Doug Niven. He had discovered the Cambodian portraits from Toul Sleng, the Khmer Rouge interrogation and death center in Phnom Penh. Those killing fields and the portraits of people awaiting the certainty of a painful death left an indelible stamp on Doug's psyche, resolved by digging, then pursuing Vietnam's take on its own history and suffering.

For those of us who passed through it, Indochina is still full of unaccountable ghosts. The legacy of images taken by Western photojournalists tends to compliment our bravado, our expeditionary self, the need to justify cause. The other side, the North, had a simpler task: They were on the defensive until the latter stages of the conflict. Their mission was to document the nationalistic cause, the heroic, however grim it had become. To prove to themselves and to their fraternal allies that their cause was righteous. In that, they have prevailed.

AS WITH OTHER THINGS IN VIETNAM, photography came courtesy of the French colonialists. In the 1840s, at about the same time that a Frenchman named Louis Daguerre perfected a way of capturing images on copper plates, a French fleet was deployed to the waters off Indochina. A quarter century later France had taken Saigon, and French Indochina was a colony in the making. Vietnam had been through this before, with China, its northern neighbor. In the centuries of Chinese dynastic domination, Vietnam's literature had been continually destroyed as a means of eradicating the broader Vietnamese culture.

Throwing off their northern neighbor's shackles over the epochs gave the Vietnamese the experience they later used against the French, the Japanese, and the Americans. They had learned to be warriors and assimilators, taking en passant from their foreign masters Confucian precepts and mandarin attitudes, the crafts and cultures they found useful, then adapting them into a uniquely Vietnamese blend.

The Vietnamese understood that French domination and the Western impact on Indochina had brought innovations worth exploiting. In 1868, a mandarin scholar, painter, and poet named Tru An was sent to Shanghai and Hong Kong, then the centers of Western influence in that sphere, to learn the new skills of photography. When he returned to Hanoi in 1869, he set up the first photo studio and shop on the street of traditional medicines. Almost any trace of Tru An's work is gone. All that has been discovered is a faded ink sketch of him posed in a high-backed

chair and an impression made of his first glass plate, a portrait of a seated mandarin. Of the original print there is no trace, and the glass plate itself has been lost, looted perhaps as a spoil of colonial power. Traditionally, copyright and ownership stayed with the family, but no descendants of Tru An can recall the plate's whereabouts. The search for it, abetted by historians and archival experts, was not to be rewarded.

In Vietnam, photography has reflected, over its short history, the long cultural tradition of portraiture. Before the days of photography, portraits—of groups, families, individuals—were done in pen and ink, and even after photography became an accepted art form, images were often patiently hand tinted. In Vietnam's blend of Confucianism, Taoism, and Buddhism, veneration of ancestors is intertwined with respect for elders, the family, the land of the family, its lineage and tutelage. To the Vietnamese, portraits had—and still have—spiritual presence. Images of deceased relatives are part of cemetery headstones and likenesses are displayed in every household shrine. The exodus of two million since the war has not prevented émigrés from dutifully returning home to pay homage at their ancestors' shrines and grave sites. Tradition continues.

Photography began to spread through Vietnam with the return of revolutionary photographer Khanh Ky from exile in France in the 1920s. His Paris photo shop had been a

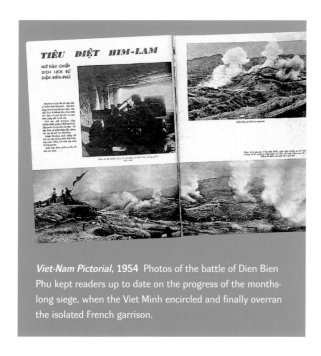

Viet-Nam Pictorial, 1954 Photos of the battle of Dien Bien Phu kept readers up to date on the progress of the months-long siege, when the Viet Minh encircled and finally overran the isolated French garrison.

haven for the other like-minded young Vietnamese revolutionaries who had found their way to the city. (One of them, a young intellectual then calling himself Nguyen Ai Quoc— Nguyen the Patriot—would eventually return to Vietnam as Ho Chi Minh.) Khanh Ky himself returned to his home village, Lai Xa, not far from the capital, in 1924 and began training photographic apprentices. Soon photography shops and studios were blossoming in Hanoi. The owners of these shops and their darkroom apprentices came from Khanh Ky's village. More shops, equipped with French cameras and materials, proliferated in the Indochina Peninsula, most producing traditional portrait photography.

In the 1920s, there was also an increase in anti-French activities countrywide. As opposition grew, the French bore down, repressing dissidents and often exiling them to other colonies around the world. As the groundswell for liberation grew, the first revolutionary tracts began to appear on the streets, though they weren't yet illustrated. That would come much later with the introduction of drawings, maps, and sketches. It was almost impossible for the revolutionary movement to find the ink and paper for its tracts, much less presses and plates. Still, that first generation of studio-trained photographers began joining the cause and documenting its progress clandestinely.

Dinh Dang Dinh, who would become one of Ho Chi Minh's personal snappers, took his first journalistic pictures at a workers demonstration in 1936. He had learned his craft at the hands of master portraitist Nguyen Van Huu, who ran the Belle Photo Studio in Hanoi. Even as a boy, Dinh had been expelled for waving a flag of the resistance at his *école supérieure.* As a young man, he had naturally flowed into the Communist Party and toward revolution. His skills in photography made him a scout in reconnaissance, snapping bridges, train stations, even French restaurants—anything that was a valid target. From 1941 to 1945 he scouted and shot classic propaganda pictures, the necessary backdrop of war.

Ho's own four years working in Khanh Ky's Paris studio had instilled in him the power of the photographic image. The need to document the young revolution was ingrained. In 1945, he asked to meet three photographers who could be assigned to him to document the revolutionary leadership. Dinh was one of them; he was joined by Trieu Dai and later Tran Cu. They became the Praetorian Guard of the new plastic arts in Vietnam. Theirs would become the globally known images.

The evolution of photography mirrored the revolution, and it found expression in print. The first news magazine, *Viet-Nam Pictorial,* appeared soon after the French defeat at Dien Bien Phu. Its first issue, out on October 11, 1954, used a combination of images poached from French sources and the first glimpses of serious combat photojournalism by Vietnamese photographers. Trieu Dai's frames of the final assault at Dien Bien Phu appeared in its pages, along with freeze frames of the battle taken from incredible 16mm footage shot by a comrade of Dai. The march into captivity of over 7,000 French POWs was similarly well documented.

The liberation of Hanoi and Ho Chi Minh's triumphant entry into the city, his review of troops in Bach Dang Square, and his address to the new nation were shot by photographers now in from the maquis—the resistance movement—where they had been covering the campaigns against the French. Nguyen Dinh Uu, Dinh Dang Dinh, and half a dozen other comrades became the staffers for the first daily papers published in North Vietnam.

With the lull in the fighting, a false sense of peace prevailed as the Geneva Accords were observed in 1954. The nation was divided at the 17th parallel, with the Democratic Republic of Vietnam in the north under Ho Chi Minh and the Republic of Vietnam in the south under Bao Dai. The accords that divided the country also divided families. For ideological, religious, or economic reasons, thousands flocked to the North, others similarly fled to the South. Photographer Mai Nam's family was typical. His father, finding himself out of work in Hanoi, headed south with his younger children. Mai Nam and his older borther stayed behind to work for the cause.

As the revolution gathered steam, it also gathered photographers. Most, even those from humble backgrounds, had the advantage of a French education. Their fluency in French gave them the basic skills and ability to consume textbooks and photographic instruction manuals. Their exposure to the tastes of their colonial masters influenced their styles. There is a French realism to their work, a brevity of composition. Not until the late fifties and early sixties, when the first Vietnamese cadres were dispatched to photojournalism courses in Moscow or Leipzig, did that style start to shift, to become more formalized, more propagandic, bleaker. Access to foreign publications also dried up at that time, and the photographers covering the home front rarely glimpsed the work of their counterparts, the Western photojournalists covering the war.

Hanoi, 1945 Massed skulls and bones testify to the famine of 1945, when between one and two million Vietnamese died as food requisitions by occupying Japanese forces coincided with devastating floods. This grisly image was a departure from the photographer's prewar subjects. As a wealthy young man, he had photographed women, flowers, and scenery.
NGUYEN DUY KIEN

Many of the elder gentlemen of Vietnamese photography, who joined the revolution in its early years, have survived to this day. Venerable old men still printing in their obsolete darkrooms, they reflect the struggle to be free of colonial rule and the endurance to reunify a nation. Their histories and their photography embody the recent history of Vietnam. Their lives are its core.

In Hanoi the widow of Nguyen Duy Kien, the North's stylistic classicist and herself a portraitist, still holds court in her chamber behind what was once that first photo shop opened by Tru An more than a century ago. Poverty and time have reduced her to a room and a half crammed with priceless antiques and gold-lacquered panels. Her husband's legacy—images of provincial life from the 1940s and '50s—are immaculately preserved, the original prints in flat binders signed and dated, the portraits redolent of the 1930s and pin sharp in their formality.

Madame Kien holds up Kien's perfectly framed prints of the destruction wrought during the fighting against the French and the further destruction caused by the 1945-46 famine in the Tonkin that claimed between one and two million people. She also has photographs showing the joys of liberation in the 1950s. That joy was brief. Three million more people would perish in the coming quarter century of war.

Despite his stature as one of the 20th century's predominant political figures, the father of Vietnamese independence remains surprisingly elusive to this day. Westerners generally recall Ho Chi Minh as a frail-looking old man with a wispy goatee—hardly the image of a wartime leader whose accomplishments on behalf of his country are on a par with those of renowned statesmen such as Winston Churchill and Franklin Roosevelt.

Who exactly was Ho Chi Minh? In a sense, he was many people, and he lived many lives.

Born in 1890 in a village in central Vietnam, Ho was originally named Sinh Cung. His mother died in 1901, and his father was fired from the bureaucracy for drunkenness and incompetence in 1908, after which he became an itinerant seller of oriental medicine. Ho grew up chafing under French colonial rule, and when he was 21 he fled his homeland. He would not return to Vietnam for 30 years. For three decades he roamed the world, leading a chameleon-like existence. He adopted a string of aliases, including Nguyen Ai Quoc—Nguyen the Patriot—Tran Luc, and Viktor. Already fluent in French, he mastered English, Russian, Thai, and at least three Chinese dialects.

Ho spent nearly three years at sea aboard French freighters, stopping at ports around the world. He lived in the United States for a while, working in Boston and as a laborer in Brooklyn. He later worked as a pastry chef in London's posh Carlton Hotel. While in London, Ho began conversing with Irish nationalists and other political activists. From London, he moved on to Paris, where he lived for six years, becoming a pamphleteer, journalist, playwright—and confirmed revolutionary.

In the salons and meeting halls of Paris in the 1920s, Ho mingled with socialists and communists who fueled his nationalist fervor. Working to achieve an independent, communist Vietnam would become Ho's focus for the remainder of his days. His dedication to that cause

OPPOSITE

Near Dong Khe, 1950
Assisted by Chinese advisors, Ho observes a battle between French and Viet Minh forces from a mountain command post along the Vietnam-China border. Ho's cause was bolstered in 1949 when the communists took control of China and began providing the Viet Minh with modern weapons and other support.

DINH DANG DINH

Hanoi, Oct. 11, 1945
Brig. Gen. Philip E. Gallagher arrives in Hanoi to help accept the surrender of the Japanese, who had occupied Vietnam during WWII. To Gallagher's left stand Ho Chi Minh and Emperor Bao Dai. During the war, Ho had good relations with the U.S. and hoped to gain its support for Vietnamese independence, which he had declared on Sept. 2, 1945.

PHOTOGRAPHER UNKNOWN

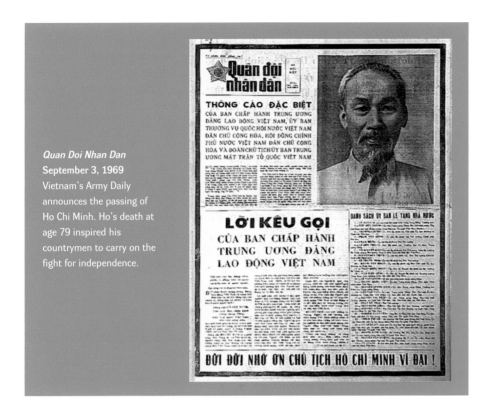

took him to Moscow, where he met Stalin and other Soviet leaders, as well as to China. He proselytized among Vietnamese expatriate communities in China and Thailand. He was imprisoned in China and Hong Kong. He suffered from tuberculosis, malaria, and amoebic dysentery.

In 1941, Ho returned to Vietnam to oppose both the French colonial regime and Japanese occupation forces. It was at this time that he adopted the name by which he is known to posterity, Ho Chi Minh—Bringer of Light. His homecoming was inauspicious—his initial base of operations was a cave near Pac Bo in the north of Vietnam on the Chinese border. But as the leader of the communist-dominated independence movement, the Viet Minh, Ho saw his power and influence grow steadily.

Because of their resistance against the Japanese, the Viet Minh received arms and funding from the United States, which led Ho to hope for U.S. support for Vietnamese independence. After the first covert OSS (Office of Strategic Services) teams were inserted into northern Vietnam in 1945, Ho reportedly asked their commander to provide him with a copy of the American Declaration of Independence, along with a carton of Lucky Strikes. U.S. support was not to be, however, and the return of the French to power in Indochina following WWII led to three more decades of fighting in Vietnam.

Although Ho guided his country through eight years of war against the French and through the early years of conflict with South Vietnam and its American supporters, he would not live to see the reunification of Vietnam. He died in 1969. His body was embalmed, and in 1975 it was placed in a mausoleum in Hanoi that was modeled on Lenin's tomb. Thousands of Vietnamese and other tourists now file through the mausoleum every year, most of them to bow in respect at the foot of Ho's glass sarcophagus.

To most Vietnamese, Ho Chi Minh was a combination of George Washington and Thomas Jefferson. A bachelor who seldom made contact with his own family after leaving home as a young man, this mysterious figure came to be regarded as a family member by millions of Vietnamese. To gauge the reverence in which he is still held, one need look no further than Vietnam's paper currency, the dong, every denomination of which bears the portrait of one man and one man alone: Bac Ho—Uncle Ho.

Location unknown, 1953
Ho meets with party and military leaders to plan the campaign against the French at Dien Bien Phu. The "four pillars" of the Vietnamese Communist Party included Ho, Pham Van Dong, Truong Chinh, and Gen. Vo Nguyen Giap, who led the Viet Minh in their climactic victory at Dien Bien Phu.
DINH DANG DINH

Hanoi, May 19, 1955
Ho Chi Minh inspects the Hoang Ngan militia unit at Bach Mai military airport shortly after the French were ousted from Vietnam. During the Indochina War, this unit, from the Hai Duong area east of Hanoi, protected National Highway 5, the vital link between the North Vietnamese capital and Haiphong, the North's major port.
NGUYEN DINH UU

DINH DANG DINH

In 1974, I was assigned to go south to take photographs of the Ho Chi Minh Trail and one of its major branches, Route 9, in southern Laos. I had been in the South for almost a year and had worked the trail's entire length. The trail was historically important and needed to be documented. Some of my colleagues had worked there, but very few had had pictures of the trail published.

During the course of my journey I used three cameras and took nearly a hundred rolls of film, including many wonderful pictures of the north-to-south supply line.

We were in the jungle most of the time and under bombardment. When you saw a plane, all you could do was run for cover. One day enemy aircraft dropped bombs right on top of us near Loc Ninh (at the southern end of the trail just north of Saigon near the Cambodian border). It was so bad I had to abandon my equipment and run. If I had tried to save my gear, I would have lost my life. But in an instant I lost all my work. It was all destroyed, everything. I even lost my sandals and my hat. All I had left were my shirt and pants. I was lucky to have escaped. A few days later I went back to look for my camera and film. All I found were strips of exposed film and a few pieces of cloth hanging from the branches of trees. The airplanes had dropped white phosphorous and napalm bombs that burned everything, leaving nothing behind. My film had already been exposed to the light, so there was no way of retrieving it. I never knew what happened to my cameras, they simply disappeared. When I finally returned to Hanoi empty-handed, government officials told me not to worry about the lost material. They said that I was lucky to be alive. You should have no regrets, they told me. But I was so consumed by regret that I couldn't sleep for several months. I had made such a huge sacrifice and had nothing to show for it. You know, I still lose sleep over the loss.

The highlight of my career was being Chairman Ho Chi Minh's personal photographer. Chairman Ho's not with us anymore, but I want to tell you something: During the U.S. bombing of North Vietnam, he never left, never evacuated. He stayed at his home in Hanoi. For some reason no bombs ever fell within a one-kilometer radius of his home. The Party and government buildings were never hit either; it could have been deliberate not to hit our brain center during the time of war. The whole city had already been evacuated. But Ho, the party leaders, and government officials decided to stay. Since Ho stayed, so did I. But we didn't have any problems.

I joined the (anti-French) resistance in 1936. When Ho set up an anti-Japanese base at Pac Bo (near the rugged Chinese border) in 1941, I was allowed to start photographing the political activities of the resistance. While he was living in the northern mountains, Ho asked us to build him a simple house on stilts near a stream in which he liked to bathe. He wanted to be close to the people and live simply, but he also wanted the location of his house to remain secret. He had a large piece of land where he grew crops and played sports like volleyball.

Then, one month after Ho declared Vietnam's independence from France on September 2, 1945, in Hanoi, I had the honor to make the first official portrait of him. At the time, I didn't know that Chairman Ho was the great patriot Nguyen Ai Quoc, whom we had all heard about. Had I known that, it could have been a different type of portrait. Anyway, the purpose of the portrait was that it be distributed to the public to publicize Ho's identity. We made enlargements of the portrait, which were sent all over the country. During the tumultuous events of 1945 and all of 1946 I stayed in Hanoi taking pictures, even of Ho's meetings with France's colonial commanders. I didn't go to France with Ho that year, but I was in Haiphong to photograph him when he returned in October 1946.

Hanoi, 1960 Ho Chi Minh writes commendation letters in the garden of the Presidential Palace. Ho abjured the palace in favor of a simple two-room stilt house nearby. The photographer recalls that Ho never evacuated his house despite the U.S. bombing. "For some reason no bombs ever fell within a one kilometer radius of his home."

DINH DANG DINH

Soon afterward, when war broke out with the French, I photographed the French attacks on Lang Son and Haiphong in November 1946. By December I was assigned to fight against the French in Section 3 of Hanoi, working as a reconnaissance photographer. The street fighting was so intense that I was lucky to survive. We captured and held Kham Thien and Hang Bot Streets until we received orders to retreat. But when I got separated from my unit, I thought that it would be useful for me to stay quietly behind in Hanoi to document the people's keen support of Ho's resistance movement. Then, in 1948, came the big surprise for me. The (Vietnam Workers') Party's General Secretary came to Hanoi and asked me to follow him up north to take pictures of the big guys. Suddenly, there I was in the Party's Central Office, taking pictures of Ho, a job that lasted until the day he died in 1969.

There is something special about my photos from the resistance time. Everything was difficult. We had no electricity. There was an economic blockade on resistance-controlled zones, making it almost impossible for us to get paper and film from Hanoi. But Chairman Ho said he needed photographs of himself to hand out as presents to visitors. I told Ho that with no power and nothing to work with, it would take me several days to make some prints. "Obstacles make you clever," Ho replied.

So I made a darkroom in a dirt bunker, built a wooden enlarger onto which I fit my camera's lens, and then used the sunlight from a small hole in the roof. For containers, we used a type of big bamboo. To wash photographs, we took sections of bamboo, cut them in half, and covered them with beeswax. We also washed film and photographs in a nearby stream, which gave better results than when we washed them in well water. All the photographs from those nine years in the mountains with the resistance are still unspoiled. There must have been minerals such as calcium in the water that helped to preserve the film.

Hanoi, 1946 A Vietnamese orphan stands amid the rubble of his orphanage, bombed by French reoccupation forces following their return to power in Vietnam after WWII. The photographer's wife recalls that he took this photograph to document "the abominable French scorched-earth policy."

NGUYEN DUY KIEN

OPPOSITE

Bac Can Province, 1950 Viet Minh soldiers cross a bamboo pontoon bridge erected during the Bien Gioi campaign against the French. Although the action took place nine years before the advent of the Ho Chi Minh Trail, this precursor to the trail demonstrates construction techniques that would be used in the fight against the Americans.

PHOTOGRAPHER UNKNOWN

Dien Bien Phu, 1954 Viet Minh soldiers rest between battles in one of the hundreds of miles of trenches that protected them from enemy fire during the two-month siege of the French garrison, located on the Laotian border west of Hanoi. The fall of Dien Bien Phu to Gen. Vo Nguyen Giap's forces marked the beginning of the end of the French occupation of Indochina.

PHOTOGRAPHER UNKNOWN

Haiphong, August 1955 A Viet Minh commander and his French
counterpart discuss plans for the last French forces to leave Vietnam at
the end of the war. France's rule of Vietnam, which began in 1859, had
come to a bloody end. More than 35,000 French soldiers died in the
Indochina War, and Vietnamese casualties were even higher.

NGUYEN DINH UU

Hanoi, October 9, 1954 Vanquished French soldiers depart Hang Dau barracks following the Geneva Accords, which partitioned Vietnam at the 17th parallel pending a nationwide vote to achieve political reconciliation. The South, however, refused to participate in the election and a new phase of Indochina strife began.

NGUYEN DINH UU

NGUYEN DINH UU

My first big assignment was around 1947, photographing French POWs during our war of resistance against the French colonials. I was working for a local resistance newspaper when my guerrilla unit captured several French soldiers. We decided we should photograph them and use their images in propaganda leaflets in an effort to get French soldiers to desert their units.

It wasn't easy. At the time, we had no darkroom facilities and had to process and print our crude photographs right there in the jungle, on rocks. I was a neophyte at photography. As a young man I had played at photography with a few friends who had cameras, but I had neither a camera nor any skill, only determination. We photographed the POWs, made prints, and then spread the pictures around in the French-controlled hills so the French soldiers could see them. The photos were captioned: "With this photo in hand, come over to a friend."

When the Americans arrived in 1965, I joined *Bao Anh Viet-Nam (Viet Nam Pictorial)*. Like many photographers, I worked both as an infantry fighter and photographer. I covered the Vinh Linh region just north of the Ben Hai River, the demarcation line separating the North from the South. Vinh Linh is largely coastal sand dunes and low hills, which were flattened by U.S. bombs.

My job was to capture on film the lives and the fighting spirit of the local people who had been forced to move underground to survive the terrible American bombardment. From the start of the bombing, old people and children were evacuated to the mountains. Only the militia forces, both men and women, stayed behind to fight the enemy and to till the rice fields. To protect themselves, people had to dig tunnels deep under the sand and the hills. The trenches and tunnels connected one village to another. It was dangerous. At times, bombs and shells fell right on tunnel entrances. When it was calm, people would emerge from underground to farm. But when they were aboveground they always had to be conscious of where the nearest tunnel entrance was. When the air-raid siren wailed, everyone quickly ducked back underground. Militiamen saved me on several occasions by quickly leading me to the nearest tunnel

entrance. Otherwise I would have been lost. We took heavy fire from American aircraft and also from naval gunfire and from the U.S. artillery base at Con Thien, which was located just on the south side of the river from Vinh Linh. We suffered casualties, but not too many.

Life in the tunnels was not all that bad. We had flashlights and oil lamps. Living in such close quarters, we all became close friends. I was a brother to those people, and I shared their lives, happiness, and suffering. Wherever I went, it was like that. Sometimes I lived with a unit for months. I lived with the soldiers and the people. I made many friends with whom I had close, emotional bonds. That's the only way to make good photos: to be close to and to love and respect the people you're photographing.

To get a work of art that could be used for publishing or propaganda, you had to be on the lookout all the time. Perhaps my proudest moment came when I visited an antiaircraft unit manning 37-mm guns on Con Co island, just off the coast, which was honeycombed with tunnels like Vinh Linh. I remember the danger as American planes came roaring right at the gunners, who didn't flinch. The soldiers were ready to fight anytime night and day. My task as a photographer seemed trivial compared with theirs. The gunners stood there and fired at the diving planes, and I stood right behind them shooting pictures. I suppose we were all afraid of being killed. But fear is normal. We were all frightened. But when we put our minds to our tasks, the fear seemed to disappear. We relied on each other. Since everyone was in the same dangerous situation, sacrificing one's life seemed almost normal. In fact, the collective fight dwarfs any personal feelings. I suppose the same could be said for American war protesters who felt stronger when they demonstrated by the thousands.

Cao Bang, 1953
Photographer Uu carries all of his equipment by bicycle as he travels back to Hanoi. He had taken his very first photograph just five years earlier, when he helped capture a French detachment and used the soldiers' own camera to document the incident.
NGUYEN DINH UU

OPPOSITE

Gia Lam, 1969
Rallying popular support for the war effort, Uu created this propaganda illustration, which later appeared on a postage stamp. Entitled "Heroic Soldier from Antiaircraft Company #5 Loads Artillery Shell," the photograph was made in a suburb of Hanoi where no artillery battles ever took place.
NGUYEN DINH UU

The people and the soldiers always did their best to protect us. Our soldiers usually escorted me when I moved from one place to another on the island. The protection was pretty efficient. They'd signal the arrival of U.S. planes by firing one shot in the air. That warning would send us scrambling for the nearest tunnel.

My missions in Vinh Linh generally lasted one to two months. Then I'd take my work back to Hanoi, traveling the 560 kilometers by bicycle under constant bombardment from U.S. planes. The journey usually took 20 days. The roads were bad and most of the bridges had been knocked out. As I rode my bike, I tried to avoid traveling through the most targeted places, and I moved only at times when there seemed to be lulls in the bombing. For the smoothest ride, I tried to follow in the tire tracks of cars. If I was lucky and there was a pause in the bombing, I'd hitch a ride on a truck. Militias stationed along the roads always gave us encouragement and timely information on the bombing. They made traveling almost fun. So, everyone contributed to my photographs: the people of Vinh Linh, the militias and soldiers along the road, everyone.

While on the road I had to watch out not only for my life but also for my equipment. I couldn't play at photography anymore. We had to be extremely careful because we had very limited amounts of film that had been distributed to us by our paper. For us, one photo was like a bullet. We had to carefully choose our shots. Even if you had money, there was no place to buy film if you ran out. We were fighting against rich America, which had plenty of bombs, bullets, and film. Vietnam, being poor, had to be economical.

Young photographers work differently now. They have modern technology and transportation. They arrange everything in advance. I used to arrive without notice. I lived and ate with the people. I shared the people's hardships and suffering. Now photographers eat and stay in hotels. They have no attachment to their subjects. Now you have to financially compensate the subject you photograph. It's a different sort of emotion. When you are alongside each other in combat, feeling one for all and all for one, it's almost like love and affection. When the Americans dropped their bombs so intensely, destroying everything, it drew us closer together in adversity. I remember an old lady on Con Co island who refused to be evacuated, choosing to stay with the soldiers and do her only job: mending the flag every time it got torn by enemy fire.

THE HOME FRONT: A HOUSE DIVIDED

CHAPTER TWO

Not since the Civil War had the United States suffered a war on its own soil. Not, that is, until Vietnam came home to the streets and campuses of downtown America. Initially, the war entered the U.S. in photographs, but as communications picked up with the escalation of the conflict, more American men and women were sucked into the "green machine"—the military—and battles were played out across the nation's TV screens. Relatives and loved ones died in living color over breakfast.

In Vietnam, the war was on two home fronts. Up North the fight was against aerial and naval bombardment—and starvation. A struggle to keep a nation going on a shoestring, with every man, woman, and child working around the clock. Everyone had a job defending the nation, putting out fires from bombardments, serving the cause. In the South, the front was everywhere. Any village, any paddy field, any home could suddenly become the front line. The American military kept track of the shifting front on a computer that spit out colored combat maps, with zones from pink to red, as the enemy's areas of influence waxed and waned. The population of the South was being internally displaced by the war, refugees in their own land.

Hai Duong, 1967
Militia women guard the Lai Vu Bridge, halfway between Hanoi and the port of Haiphong on National Highway 5. Both Hanoi and Haiphong were bombed extensively in 1967. Militia units, consisting mostly of men and women unfit for army duty, played a vital role in the North, capturing nearly all of the downed U.S. pilots.
MAI NAM

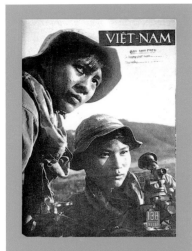

On both fronts, every outgoing round of fire became somebody's incoming. Since there were no traditional front lines, or only occasional ones at the siege of a base like Khe Sanh, the war, the violence, could erupt anywhere. It could be a Viet Cong bomb in the heart of downtown Saigon, outside a bar or hotel; an incoming rocket landing on a church; an artillery round plummeting into a peasant's thatched hut; a gunship pilot maniacally pumping his minigun at a water buffalo herd. It could be a booby trap, a B-52 air strike, unseen, unheard from 38,000 feet above the capital suburbs on Christmas Day. It could happen so, in the blink of an eye. The whole of Indochina was on edge, paranoid, petrified, and alienated.

Those in the North took comfort in their fear, believing that their nationalist cause was just. It was for them a total war, with the homeland under continuous bombardment, a civilian population with no place to run. Death was not something unexpected, more something worth confronting, for the cause was righteous and to die for it was not in vain. It was a sacrifice to be made for the future of family and country. Patriotic fervor was evident from start to finish in the photographs, whether they showed the victory against the French in '54 or a group heading off down the Ho Chi Minh Trail in '74. There was an implicit hope and belief embedded in the photographs—that the war would end, that there would be peace.

In the South, hope and despair ebbed and flowed as the war raged on and the Saigon regime coerced and taxed its inhabitants into a submission that, when not obeyed, brought the wrath of the military machine through their backyards. The repression only created more sympathizers for the Northern-backed National Liberation Front.

Everyone caught in this theater of war became a victim by default. Not least the photographers. They couldn't just glaze through their experiences, using the lens as a veil for defusing the horror around them. And there was a beauty in those images of horror, an aspect of Goya or Brueghel. A macabre surreal thing, too awesome to be real. The inhumanities these photographers observed seemed even more poignant frozen as pictures than they did at the moment of exposure. On the home front you were exposed to death or mutilation at any second, at any place, most chillingly in your own home.

The photos the Western press sent back home fueled the antiwar fire. A new generation was chanting, "Hell, no, we won't go." Ho Chi Minh and Che Guevara became the icons of resistance, pulsed on by the continual beat of rock and roll and protest songs. The fire was lit.

Hanoi knew this, and, as we learned, we in the Western media led a semiprotected existence. The North kept track of our movements, our bureaus and houses were infiltrated and we now know there were edicts not to shoot the *bao chi* (press). Relatively few of us were shot or wounded by line-of-fire weapons. In the heyday of the mid-sixties, we could arrange to get captured for a few days, then come out of captivity with a very syndicatable piece. We had mobility. It was always possible, well almost, to get on your Honda or Yamaha motorbike and ride to another town, certain precautions observed. The main ones: Don't travel with military vehicles, and don't be the first down the road in the morning or the last at night.

The game of hide-and-seek played by the North Vietnamese photographers was in

and out of the shadows. They wore the ubiquitous green fatigues or black cotton paja-mas. Should they be caught by ARVN (the South Vietnamese Army) or U.S. troops, they could expect no mercy, no leniency, no quarter. They were the enemy. The North lost hundreds of press personnel. Often a mixed crew of photojournalists, writers, filmfolk, and propagandists would take off for the South in a truck and get caught in a B-52 strike on the Ho Chi Minh Trail. Dinh Dang Dinh talks tremblingly of just such an encounter, after finishing a fruitful 100-roll shoot in the South. His unit was caught in such an attack, and when he came to, he was naked except for his underwear, con-cussed, his eardrums broken. Shreds of his film hung in the trees. Concussion waves from an attack like that seemed to pitch you across the sky.

Van Bao recounts being dispatched to cover the B-52 bombings of Haiphong in '72. The raids swept across the North during the Christmas observances, an attempt to bring the North to the peace table. An added gambit was the mining of the North's harbors. The B-52s were met by a hail of SAMs (surface-to-air missiles) and by a few brave MIG-21 pilots. The strike hit the eastern flank of the port. Bao and a colleague from the Viet-nam News Agency managed to get to the eastern suburbs of the city, to Thuong Ly township and its bridge. Beyond that, the bombing had been devastating, there seemed nothing else alive, save the two of them and their driver. As daylight came, Bao shot staggering pictures of a sole survivor and his dead sons. The man had lost all 17 family members. Retelling the story almost 30 years later, Van Bao was reduced to tears.

Bao had joined the liberation army as a photographer in 1950, at the age of 20. His first camera was a French box camera with a 35mm fixed lens. During the French war, Van Bao learned to process and print his film under primitive conditions in the Viet Bac,

Binh Chanh, March 1967
Two young Viet Cong (right) take a break along the Saigon River on the outskirts of Saigon. The photographer (left) sits beside a guerrilla radio operator in the same area in 1971. Actually a reporter, Am took only one roll of film, 70 shots, during the entire war. "I didn't have extra film and didn't know how to change the rolls."

TRAM AM

Viet-Nam Pictorial, **1967** The image at left by photographer Mai Nam celebrated the role of village militia. Such stories played up patriotism by lauding the wartime contributions of civilians as well as the military.

the resistance heartland. After the '54 peace accords, he was given a better camera and a job with the government's agricultural newspaper for three years. Poached from there by the burgeoning Vietnam News Agency, he was lucky, early in the war, to get pictures of some of the first downed American pilots in the panhandle province of Quang Binh. His images of Air Force major Robert H. Shumaker were seen around the world. Bao's presence, with his camera, at the POW camp could even stop the harassment of prisoners. His other trophy scoop portrayed the capture of another pilot being transported to prison on a water buffalo sled. Van Bao's front was as close to home as anyone would care for, and he was lucky to have escaped unscathed.

THE PHOTOGRAPHERS WORKING FOR THE LIBERATION NEWS SERVICE in the South spent virtually their entire time living clandestinely. Theirs was a role akin to the resistance groups that had operated in occupied Europe during World War II. The skills they had honed during the Viet Minh resistance to the French were resharpened. Tunnel systems, started in the mid-1950s on the scarps and plateaus northwest of Saigon, were enlarged, becoming a network that would eventually stretch 120 miles. In certain places, as at Cu Chi, the tunnel complex penetrated U.S. divisional bases. Offensives aimed at the capital and its chain of encircling American bases were launched from this zone. The area infiltrated by the tunnel system would never be secure. The Vietnamese resistance went underground and moved by night. It was impossible to distinguish friend from foe; any civilian not carrying a valid government ID card risked at best interrogation, or worst arrest, torture, and relocation.

One of the liberation press working clandestinely in the South, Vo Anh Khanh, had started out as a farmer in Ca Mau, then learned photo skills as an assistant in a photo shop in Saigon. Later he operated his own small shop in the Mekong Delta town of Bac Lieu for two years, in '58 and '59, until his brother's arrest drove him to join the front and to help its cause through his images. Those images were never published in a newspaper, but they did hang in mangrove swamps and coconut groves, inspiring the committed. Folks would come from miles away to see the exhibition and hear the evening's talk about the fight, the revolution, the doctrine as passed down from Hanoi, tales of local and faraway heroism.

Khanh spent most of his time like other liberation photographers, preoccupied with day-to-day survival activities—farming, moving the wounded, bringing up supplies, or fighting. He never had the luxury of being simply an observer. Having Khanh away at the front put a double strain on his wife, who had to stay home to look after their two children. Every few months Khanh managed to get home for a night or two, or his wife would smuggle herself off to the swamps, bringing badly needed photo and medical supplies.

Movement was a nighttime affair. Khanh's images of a MASH unit performing brain surgery in the swamps are chillingly haunting. The operating table is set on poles with mosquito nets hung with strips of tire tubes, as in Ho Chi Minh sandal thongs. At any moment the unit might have to take down their facility, pack it all on boats, and pole off to a more secure area.

Just as we Western photographers could be stuck in a firefight 60 feet from the action, so could our Vietnamese counterparts. It could be frustrating. But by guile and guesswork and a good shake of Lady Luck, you might find yourself in the wrong place at the right time, even on your day off. Mai Nam got lucky in 1967 and captured an F-105 plunging to Earth, with its parachuting pilot alongside. Running behind locals, he was cheated of getting shots of the pilot's arrest, as an unpassable stream of onlookers blocked him. The Vietnam News Agency turned the plane image into a greeting card that same year.

For the VNA shooters, there was no day off, unless they were wounded. The war never stopped and the home front always needed coverage. They shot frames of ordinary citizens going about their daily business, working in factories, on farms, in mines and ammo plants, or just plain living.

By this time, the war industry had retreated into caves. The Red and Black River Deltas are ringed with limestone outcrops, and even today, when you take the train from Hanoi to Ho Chi Minh City, you can see spur tracks curving off behind limestone karsts, the tracks rusted and unmarked on any map—except a U.S. Air Force one. These redoubts housed maintenance shops for transport and weaponry, and the fabrication of basic material for clothing continued in the caves, the workers often emerging to farm paddies and vegetable gardens by moonlight. Generators provided power, as power plants had been among the first casualties of the initial wave of attacks from Operation Rolling Thunder, a massive American bombing campaign begun in 1965. Those continual attacks mobilized the entire Northern population to keep the war effort rolling.

At the closest point to the demilitarized zone, on the first ridge of high ground, the North went underground again. The tunnels of Vinh Linh and Vinh Moc became symbols of the nation's resistance. Offshore, the islands that had sparked the Gulf of Tonkin incidents harbored strategic radio and radar facilities with their attendant protection. The needed resupply for them came out of the Vinh Moc tunnels and was ferried across in wooden boats. The caves were enlarged into living and logistics bunkers. Children here went to school in subterranean classrooms, getting to them along a trench system reminiscent of those in Flanders Fields. The kids wore thick, rafia-brimmed hats to protect them from falling antiaircraft shrapnel. Even the water buffaloes and pigs had their own individual revetments.

The caves were a fertile photogenic killing ground; getting to them was fraught at best. Nguyen Dinh Uu and Mai Nam managed to do it by bicycle, possibly the safest way. Truck convoy trips could likely end in rocket attacks. Mai Nam survived one such direct hit while waiting at a ferry crossing. Back in the tunnels, he pioneered a primitive lighting system to take the place of a modern flash unit. He carefully emptied an AK-47 cartridge onto a square of paper, laid it on the floor, posed his subjects, braced himself against the wall with his camera on time exposure, then ignited the paper. The technique produced a soft-sharp, evocative Victorian-like image. One of his memorable images from the caves showed a group of militia women, who farmed and fought in shifts. Female crews manned the antiaircraft batteries, while those out farming the paddies stacked

Khe Sanh, May 9, 1973
Cuban leader Fidel Castro hoists a victory flag at the site of the strategic 1968 battle just south of the DMZ. The siege of Khe Sanh was part of the North's plan to divert U.S. and South Vietnamese forces from population areas prior to the Tet offensive, a massive assault that undermined American support for the war.
NGOC KHANH

Viet-Nam Pictorial, 1967 A story on downed U.S. pilots featured the photo at left in which a diminutive militia woman guards a hulking American, an image later made into a postage stamp (below).

their rifles close by to take on low-flying aircraft in a hail of lead from behind the dikes.

For any photographer with a touch of claustrophobia, covering the tunnels was a nightmare. Unless you really liked tunnels. At every level of society, North and South, life was interrupted with long spasms underground. The tunneling that had started with the Viet Minh resistance in the French period was extended. From the Cu Chi complex to the network astride the Cambodian border, every village and hamlet had a system of house bunkers and communication trenches. All approaches were studded with fiendishly devastating booby traps. Whole communities would turn out en masse to sharpen bamboo *punji* sticks to place in camouflaged pits near cave entrances. In the tunnels themselves, baskets of snakes and scorpions sprang open in blind corners. The U.S. "tunnel rats" sent in to chase Charlie out sometimes met fates in those underground honeycombs that are still unknown.

For the Vietnamese as well, the tunnels could be deathtraps when collapsed by air strikes. Duong Thanh Phong, now the curator of the National Liberation Front's photojournalism collection, dug himself out of tunnels twice. Four of his immediate family were not so lucky. Getting out of any bunker after an attack was a blessing; few photographers escaped injury, and a near hit was casually brushed aside. They got no medals for wounds. Even today Phong remembers with pride his title of champion digger. "You had to dig for your life."

Conditions out in the swamps and jungles were just as horrific. For the Vietnamese photographers, darkrooms as we know them were an impossibility, transmission by any form electronic nonexistent. Tran Binh Khoul, who worked with Vo Anh Khanh up on the Cambodian border, took images of a night attack by powering his flash with a car battery carried on his back. Back at liberation press headquarters, even then sporadically on the move through the South, the Vietnam News Agency folks and front service teams were lucky enough to have their own personal bunker. A primitive printing facility enabled them to print black-and-white images, so that photo exhibitions, reminiscent of the newspapers on the walls of Mao's China, could be hung—as Vo Anh Khanh's were—in mangrove swamps and forests. A few small party broadsheets were churned out, too, and passed around to the point of disintegration. Surviving material has been preserved through individual diligence and sheer luck.

UP IN HANOI, HO MAINTAINED HIS HUMBLE, STILTED RESIDENCE on the grounds of the former governor's mansion. City parks and squares harbored bunkers, manhole covers in sidewalks led to individual shelters made from pipe sections. The dikes holding back the Red River, always under threat, bristled with antiaircraft batteries. Photographers at the VNA watched the air battles from the fifth-floor roof of their building on Hai Ba Trung Street. Lacking long lenses, they would enlarge the frames of flaming planes, then dispatch a duty snapper to another wreck being pulled apart for recycling in a suburban paddy. During the '72 Christmas bombings, a B-52 plummeted into a small lake a quarter mile from Ho's house. Its tail and part of a wing still provide a roost for the lake's duck contingent. Unfortunately, the Northern politicos only wanted to disseminate shots of humiliated enemy pilots or party press conferences to the West. By the time the Western news agencies received their packs of prints for distribution, the world press had moved on to some other, more immediate horror.

The Vietnamese newsreel cameramen endured the same hardships as the still photographers. But their task was further complicated by the sheer weight of the obsolete East German gear they used and by the necessity of getting their film back to Hanoi. From there, it was shipped to East Berlin for processing. It could take weeks to see the rushes. The cameramen also suffered nearly the same casualties as the stills lads, losing over 70 people from among their ranks during the 30-year struggle.

Tran Van Thung, a leading cinematographer, recalls being sent South in '66 with ten cans of bulk stock and told to return when he had completed shooting. What he decided to shoot would be up to him. After six months, he plodded from Quang Nam back to Hanoi, the exposed footage stored in rice bran in the container preferred by most photographers—a U.S. ammo box. The finished cut would show in Prague at the '68 film festival as *Nhang Dan Que Toi (My People, My Village)*. Dinh Dang Dinh's still photos ran in an exhibition accompanying the film when it was shown in Hanoi, alongside icons by Mai Nam and Van Bao. Other exhibitions in Eastern European cities provided the major venue for Vietnamese war imagery until wire transmissions improved in late '71.

By this time *Viet-Nam Pictorial*, the North's premier photo journal, was published for foreign distribution in English, French, German, Russian, and Japanese. But it continued to fall victim to unpredictable supplies of ink, paper, and power to run the presses. Until the closing years of the war, its photographic covers and color spreads were still being hand tinted. Paintings by older artist-photographers like The Dinh occasionally graced the magazine's covers, keeping that traditional format alive even as technology was overtaking it.

By the end of '72, with the offensive across the demilitarized zone, the home front had become the battlefront. Neither side had to dispatch its news gatherers very far to find a story. Casualties among the media fraternity swelled with the intensity of the offensive south of the My Chanh River.

By this time, in 1973, the liberation press in the South were starting to emerge from the shadows and make themselves known. They documented the four-party talks between the North, the National Liberation Front, the South, and the U.S. in Saigon. The talks resulted in a plan for American withdrawal and for the division of the country. Photographers like Lam Tan Tai, infiltrated back into the South years previously, covered the talks and the subsequent prisoner exchanges.

The war now became a land grab, each side planting its flag in as many hamlets as possible. Both parties lost more men in this negotiation period of theoretical stability than in the three preceding years. The resistance emerged to liberate remote zones, safe now that U.S. retribution from the air was no more. Up North in the mountain fastnesses, the supply trails were enlarged and repaired in a newfound security.

Photographers from every paper and publication bagged a ride to the ever creeping front. For the first time, the liberation press in the South could install wire machines north of the DMZ and at their headquarters. The frames they captured were making it onto the front pages of Hanoi newspapers within two days. The fortunes of war were changing.

Nghe An Province, July 1972
Jane Fonda visits an antiaircraft artillery unit in southern North Vietnam. Her trip angered American conservatives, who dubbed her "Hanoi Jane." Fonda's aim was to draw attention to the bombing of villages and hospitals. "She was very easygoing and wanted to be treated like a Vietnamese," recalls the photographer.
MINH DIEN

MAI NAM

I learned from the beginning that being in the resistance against the French and the Americans meant being inventive. I was a 19-year-old interested in painting, music, and playing the guitar when I joined. I was immediately assigned to help a youth group produce a clandestine newspaper. How we managed to do that in our remote and mountainous base area was incredible.

My teacher was a bright, talented cadre who loved photography. He showed me how to painstakingly carve my paintings on a wood block using a special knife and how to write backwards on rocks, using ink and pine resin. I got so adept at writing in reverse that I could write out several pages on rocks in one day. Then we'd roll the ink-soaked, wooden blocks and the rocks over the newsprint to create our crude newspaper.

My big break was when my teacher took me on as his photographer's assistant even though I didn't know anything about photography. I learned quickly. He showed me how to take pictures with his old German-made camera, how to develop film, and how to make prints from negatives. Our enlarger was a small mud hut with a tiny, square-shaped, glass-covered opening in the roof that directed a thin beam of sunlight through a bellows and a lens onto light-sensitive paper. I shot my first subjects with a precious roll of Kodak film. I was delighted when my teacher said the photos were great. But then a French attack turned my early work and our mud-hut photo lab to ashes.

With the liberation of China in 1949 our resistance became less isolated from the outside world. We began receiving supplies from China, and by 1951 I traveled to the Berlin Festival as a Vietnamese delegate to the World Youth Congress. There I bought my first camera: a German-designed, Russian-made brand called a Kiev. It was such a precious item. Cameras and film were still scarce in North Vietnam. I guarded and took care of it as if it were my own baby. But I was crushed one day when a guy scratched the lens while trying to brush out some mold.

By 1953 I had done well enough that the (Communist) Party put me in charge of seven workers. Our job was to put out a new youth publication: *Bao Tien Phong Thanh Nien (Avant-*

Hanoi, 1968

"I wanted my pictures to be a weapon," says the photographer, at right. With a style that focused on daily life, Nam brought a unique personal perspective to his work. After the war, he pioneered beauty pageant photography. Now 70, Nam lives in a home whose walls bear pictures of beautiful women, not scenes of war.

MAI NAM

OPPOSITE

Ha Tay Province, 1968

A militia woman shoulders her weapon in defense of Binh Da hamlet, one of countless villages in the North whose inhabitants answered the call to arms. The photographer, a master of depicting Vietnam's youth in heroic poses, says, "I wanted to show how resolute were the Vietnamese people, especially the young."

MAI NAM

Garde Youth Newspaper.) With our border wide-open to the north, we even got a new printing press. Still, our operation remained hidden deep in the forest for security reasons and was only accessible by bicycle. Even so, we were bombed constantly, our living conditions were dangerous and harsh, and we could only produce one issue a month. In 1954, I returned to Hanoi and became a full-time photographer for *Tien Phong*, our independent country's first paper to publish photographs. I've worked for *Tien Phong* my entire career. During the American war I tried to capture simple, everyday scenes showing how everyone lived and contributed to the national effort in ways both big and small.

We photographers never stopped innovating. When I was taking pictures near the DMZ and the Vinh Linh area in 1968, we even came up with a new form of flash photography to illuminate our fighters and villagers who were living in bomb shelters and tunnels. We emptied gunpowder from rifle cartridges onto a small handheld device and then lit the gunpowder with a match. The burning powder created all the light we needed.

Hanoi, 1972 Military trucks park in relative safety in front of the French Embassy on Tran Hung Dao Boulevard. In November 1971, however, American bombs accidentally struck the embassy. Despite massive bombing commencing in 1965, Hanoi's residents attempted to preserve normal lives. "Bombs are terrible but we still have our song," went a saying at the time.

MAI NAM

Hanoi, Aug. 1971 Eight students from a group of 109 joyfully receive the news that they were accepted into the army—a reaction far different from that of many American draftees. "At this time," said one of the photographers, "young men were chosen because they had good revolutionary credentials," which usually meant they didn't come from landowning families.

KIM HUNG

OPPOSITE

Haiphong, July 1967 New recruits undergo physical examinations. The North's volunteer system was transformed into a mandatory system in 1973, when all able-bodied males were drafted. From a corps of around 35,000 men in 1950, the NVA grew to over half a million men by the mid-'70s, a force the U.S. military conceded was one of the finest in the world.

BAO HANH

Quang Binh Province, 1969 Just above the DMZ, a ferry tows a barge of NVA soldiers across a river as they make their way south. Despite American attempts at blocking infiltration, at this stage of the war the North was able to send more than 10,000 troops a month into South Vietnam, along with adequate supplies of food and arms.

PHOTOGRAPHER UNKNOWN

OPPOSITE

Hoa Binh Province, 1974 NVA soldiers march with village children who have come out to greet them. Once a year soldiers would stay in local villages for three months in order to strengthen ties with the people. Taken just outside of Hanoi, this photograph was one of the many propaganda shots intended to rally the population to the war effort.

NGUYEN DINH UU

OPPOSITE

Thanh Tri, September 1965

Using overhead targets, a militia company practices firing ahead of speeding aircraft. Even using antiquated WWII rifles such as these, the Vietnamese were able to cripple or down many U.S. craft. This militia group, Company Number 6 of the Yen My Commune, earned the title of "Excellent Militia" three years in a row.

MINH DAO

A Shau Valley, 1974

An NVA soldier positions a Chinese-made mannequin, used to mislead the enemy. One of the Ho Chi Minh Trail's main entry points into the South from southern Laos, the A Shau Valley was the site of some of the fiercest fighting of the Vietnam War, including the 1969 Battle of Ap Bia, also known as Hamburger Hill.

HOANG KIM DANG

Soc Trang, 1973 Viet Cong guerillas in the Mekong Delta plant American-made Claymore mines upon learning that ARVN troops are approaching their area. When action threatened, "I would sometimes hide my equipment by putting it in a plastic bag and throwing it into a pond," says the photographer, a serious risk since he had no other camera or film.

LE MINH TRUONG

Ha Tay, 1970 Villagers prepare bamboo booby traps on a road in Hoa Xa hamlet, an army training village outside Hanoi. The Hoa Xa area was a military community, and photographers often came there from Hanoi to make propaganda pictures of training exercises.

PHOTOGRAPHER UNKNOWN

OPPOSITE

Haiphong, December 1967 Militia members unload ammunition at the North's main port. "During the American bombing, I took my most memorable photos," Ba recalls. "I actually shot a photo of Senator John McCain's plane falling out of the sky over Hanoi. I was proud of that photo and wanted it to convey a message of patriotism in the face of foreign invasion."

VU BA

Ca Mau Peninsula, 1972 Activists meet in the Nam Can forest, wearing masks to hide their identities from one another in case of capture and interrogation. From here in the mangrove swamps of the Mekong Delta, forwarding images to the North was difficult. "Sometimes the photos were lost or confiscated on the way," says the photographer.

VO ANH KHANH

Tien Giang River, 1974 Vietnamese women haul in heavy fishing nets on the upper branch of the Mekong River. "This was something very strange to see. It is exclusively a man's job in Vietnam, but during the war everyone had to make sacrifices and special efforts to get the job done."

LE MINH TRUONG

Hanoi, 1972 Militiamen wait for U.S. planes during the Christmas bombings, one of the heaviest air assaults of the war. Bombing had been suspended during the Paris peace talks, but President Richard Nixon ordered its resumption when the talks stalled. Even in the midst of war, the photographer's artistry shone through in his beautiful compositions.

MAI NAM

Cu Chi District, 1966 Guerrillas tunnel into the dry soil in the region known as the Iron Triangle, a Viet Cong stronghold bounded by the cities of Tay Ninh, Song Be, and Saigon. "We were forced to work, eat, and sleep underground," says the photographer of this frequent target of U.S. "search and destroy" missions. "At one time we were hit by 11 B-52 strikes, but were somehow lucky enough to survive."
DUONG THANH PHONG

DUONG THANH PHONG

I entered photography through the darkroom. I was born into a revolutionary family. My mother and father were active in the Viet Minh resistance in the South against the French and were regrouped to the North after the 1954 Geneva Convention. I stayed behind in the South. An aunt who had a small photo studio, called Photo Lux, in the town of Trang Bang, just north of Saigon,

brought me up. When I was about ten years old, I began doing darkroom work, mainly retouching photos. At about 13, I began working for the revolution, running messages for the Viet Minh around town and to neighboring villages. Because I was good in the darkroom and a trusted messenger boy, I was given even more serious underground responsibilities in 1954, such as making false South Vietnamese government identity cards for our clandestine fighters and cadres who were operating nearby in Cu Chi. I remember making a phony Saigon identity card for the Trang Bang Communist Party secretary, Hoang Le Kha, who was later arrested and executed by Ngo Dinh Diem.

While still a teenager, I witnessed the National Liberation Front taking shape and I became a part of it. I settled in Cu Chi, where I set up and headed the NLF's local photo operation. I saw the NLF's first General Assembly in Cu Chi and the famous "people's uprising" against Saigon in 1960. During that time, I developed and circulated propaganda photos that had been sent from North Vietnam. I also did the photo work for clandestine NLF newspapers. It was very dangerous work as I was operating in the middle of a Saigon-controlled town.

When the American army arrived in 1965, I could no longer live a double life and had to go to live underground with our guerrilla fighters in their tunnel complexes at Cu Chi. The time from 1965 to 1972 was the most difficult. American and Saigon soldiers committed so many atrocities on our villagers. Our people and soldiers suffered greatly and made huge sacrifices. The worst time was in 1969 after the Tet offensive the previous year. To survive, we were forced to work, eat, and sleep underground. At one time we were hit by 11 B-52 strikes, one after another, but were somehow lucky enough to survive. On the rare occasions when we did surface, we didn't wear clothes but only a cape made of a camouflage-colored material that allowed us to melt into the landscape. Above ground, constant Agent Orange spraying was a problem. This milky liquid coated us and made us sick. It killed cattle and, of course, all the trees and vegetation, everything that it touched. Under such pressure, many of us fled to the relative safety of our bases in Cambodia in 1970 and only returned a year or two later.

I was certainly not taking photos for their aesthetic appeal. I was not thinking of beauty. Burned and shattered homes and dead bodies are not pretty. Any pretense of aesthetics was replaced by our purpose of recording the war. Incredibly, my underground darkrooms—you could call them tunnel darkrooms—survived many attacks. We made several hundred prints of the best photos we took, right in our underground laboratory, and sent them to Hanoi, which distributed them, both inside and outside Vietnam.

You can't imagine the excitement we felt as we drove from Cu Chi toward Saigon in April 1975. The road was jammed with vehicles streaming into the city: our tanks, military trucks, even guerrillas riding bicycles. Nearing Saigon the road was almost impassable. It was strewn with military uniforms, weapons, and shoes that Saigon's soldiers had discarded as they ran. I'll never forget the shoes and the loud "thump, thump, thump" sound as we drove over them. I was awestruck when I saw our flags and tanks at the presidential palace. This was not a personal thing, an individual victory, like the happiness of getting married or seeing your first child born. This was a victory for the whole nation. It was big, immense—decades of war were over and we finally had peace.

Cu Chi, 1969
NLF political leader Ut Mot works in an underground office beneath a poster proclaiming "Chairman Ho taught us: Wherever an aggressor remains in our country, we must keep fighting and sweep him out." The leaders had separate bunkers to prevent mass casualties of the leadership. Only cadres and journalists were allowed to use radios, which they used to listen to Radio Hanoi, the BBC, and Radio Saigon. Ut Mot was later killed in a rocket attack.

DUONG THANH PHONG

Nam Dinh, May 12, 1972 Medics dash though fire and bomb damage to save the wounded after U.S. warplanes bombed this industrial city south of Hanoi. Nam Dinh is the capital of Nam Ha Province, a bastion of Catholicism prior to the partitioning of Vietnam in 1954, when hundreds of thousands of Catholics moved south.

DINH QUANG THANH

Hanoi, Dec. 26, 1972 A two-frame panorama depicts the accidental destruction of Kham Thien Street during the Christmas bombings. The nearby Hanoi train station was the intended target. The photographer recalls, "Many homes were destroyed, and many people died. This bombing happened at night, and we arrived on the scene in the early hours of the morning."

VAN BAO

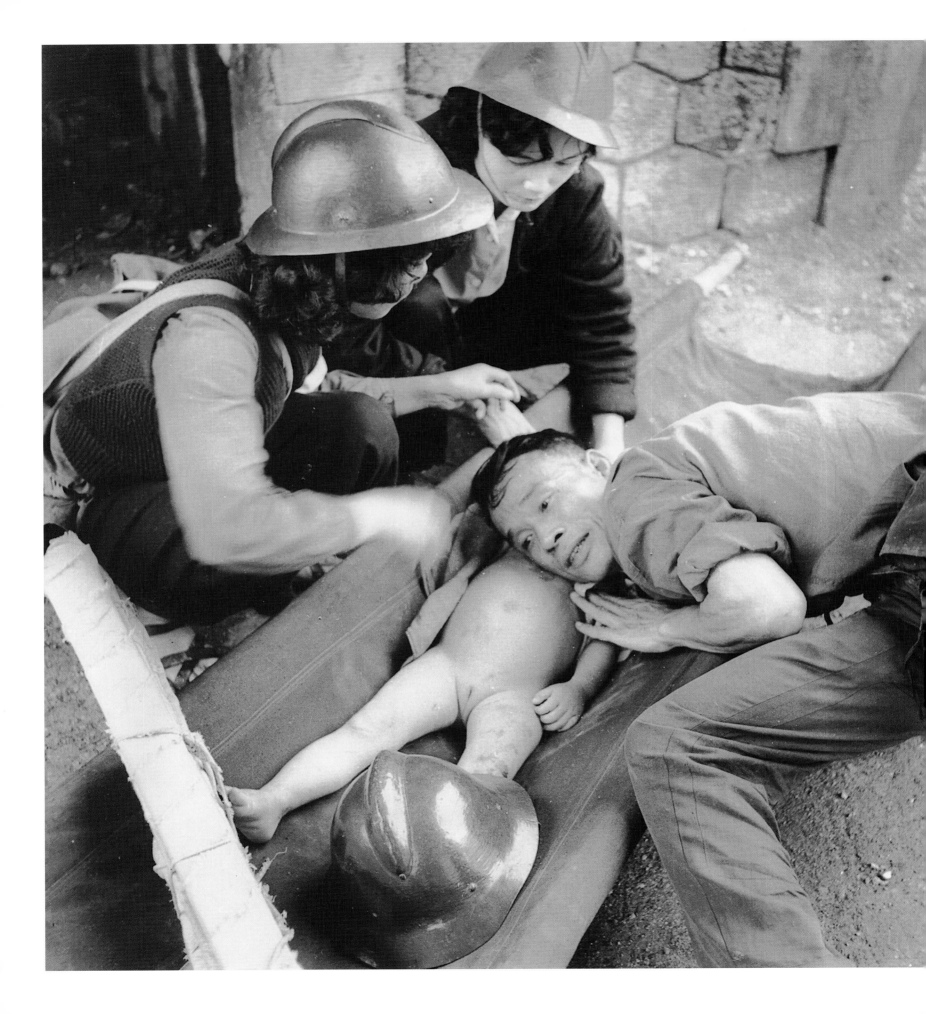

Thong Nhat, Nam Ha province, September 1972 Luong Toan, 84, walks through the rubble of Thong Nhat following U.S. bombing of the city. Luong survived a previous bombing in Thanh Hoa, farther south. National Highway 1 and the railroad both run through these cities, which made them targets of American bombs.

LAM HONG

OPPOSITE

Haiphong, December 1966 Medics treat a wounded four-year-old child after U.S. bombs fell on populated Nguyen Thiep Street. Haiphong's harbor and oil depot were main targets of American bombing attacks, although residential areas were sometimes hit. Civilian casualties were high despite the evacuation of much of the population.

LE QUANG

Hai Duong, August 8, 1972 A villager carries the lifeless body of 15-year-old Le Van Tam out of a bomb crater near Haiphong. In May, President Richard Nixon had authorized the mining of Haiphong harbor and intensified bombing of the port of Hanoi in order to pressure the North to negotiate a peace settlement at the Paris talks.

PHOTOGRAPHER UNKNOWN

Thanh Hoa, 1973 Construction workers discuss repairs of the bombed out Ham Rong Bridge, in central North Vietnam. The only route across the Ma River for heavy trucks and machinery, the bridge was heavily defended, and several U.S. planes were shot down nearby. An American MIA search team found pilot remains here.

PHOTOGRAPHER UNKNOWN

OPPOSITE

Thanh Hoa, 1973 Engineers commence repairs of the Ham Rong Bridge. Along with an adjacent power plant, the strategic bridge was destroyed and rebuilt several times, becoming a symbol of persistance to the North Vietnamese. Tinh spent most of his time either getting to the front or delivering his film back up the trail to Hanoi.

DOAN CONG TINH

Haiphong, November 19, 1967 Ly Hien Nghia, 26, is rushed to a hospital after an American bombing raid. Married only one month, Ly died from his wounds. At this stage of the war, President Lyndon Johnson offered to halt all bombing in exchange for "productive discussions" to end the fighting, although five more years of U.S. involvement would follow.

PHOTOGRAPHER UNKNOWN

Hanoi suburbs, June 1972 Militia members sort through the debris of an American plane the photographer says was downed by small-arms fire. The pilot had been flying at treetop level to avoid radar detection, but such low-flying planes were more vulnerable to small arms. U.S. planes targeted Hanoi industrial sites, but most industries were relocated to the countryside.

DOAN CONG TINH

Ca Mau Peninsula, 1972 After days of shelling a Viet Cong stronghold in the Mekong Delta, American forces leave behind a mountain of brass casings, which local villagers gather to recycle. The Vietnamese often utilized spent shells, bombs, and scrap metal from downed aircraft to fashion eating utensils and other household items.

NGUYEN VAN KIEM

South Vietnam, 1963-66 Portraits of civilian suffering: Mrs. Pham Thi Hen (opposite) lost one son and another was crippled when U.S. troops shot into the family bomb shelter. Above, clockwise from top left: Unknown elder and child; unknown woman; Le Thi Ut, 42, left with nine children after her husband was killed in a bomb shelter; Ha Van Cong, 76, burned by napalm over 60 percent of his body. An estimated 430,000 South Vietnamese civilians were killed and a million wounded between 1965 and 1974.

PHOTOGRAPHERS UNKNOWN

South Vietnam, 1968 Pham Van That, 20, from Long An Province, stands in front of a jungle people's court in an area controlled by the Viet Cong. Captured in July 1968 and charged with helping the enemy look for guerrillas and weapons, Pham was sentenced to two years imprisonment. A companion he was arrested with received the death sentence.

PHOTOGRAPHER UNKNOWN

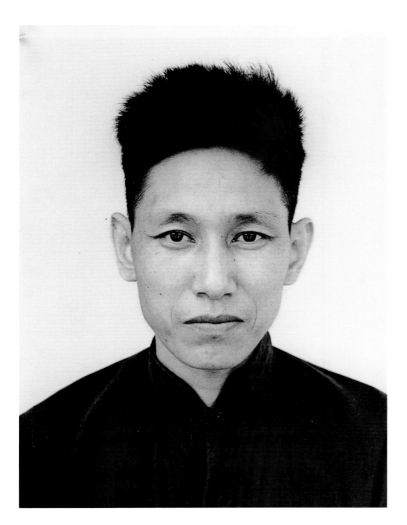

Hanoi, July 29, 1964 Four members of a South Vietnamese spy unit attempting to infiltrate the North await their fate following their capture at sea. The unsuccessful covert mission was funded by the Nationalist Chinese, South Vietnam's anticommunist ally. No such missions were ever successful, including a few directed by the CIA.

DOAN TY

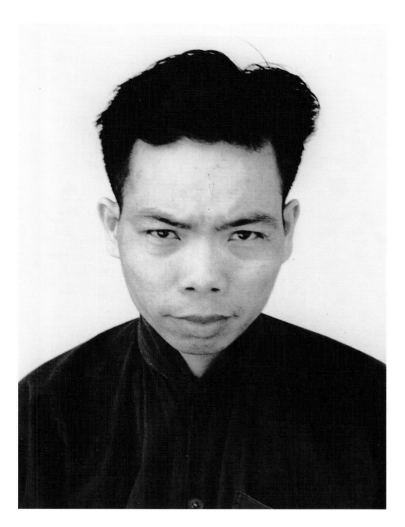

Quang Binh, February 11, 1965 Militiamen walk U.S. Navy pilot
Robert H. Shumaker away after his F8 fighter plane was shot down
near the DMZ. Recalls the photographer, "I was working with a militia
unit and I heard the news of a pilot being shot down. He wasn't hurt.
He had an imposing appearance, and I heard he had been chosen to
be a potential astronaut."

VAN BAO

Hanoi, 1973 American POWs sit on their beds in Hoa Lo Prison—
the "Hanoi Hilton"—shortly before their release on April 1, following
the withdrawal of the last American combat troops from Vietnam
after the signing of the Paris Peace Accords. The photographer made
this image on the sly, since no pictures were supposed to be taken
inside the prison.

DOAN CONG TINH

Hanoi, June 1972 U.S. Air Force Capt. Albert Molinare, captured in Thanh Hoa on April 27, 1972, sends words to his family as American POWs are presented to the Vietnamese and friendly foreign press. At war's end, 566 American military POWs and 25 civilian POWs were released, some after having served in captivity for eight years.

LAM HONG

Ca Mau Peninsula, 1968 Villagers examine revolutionary posters in a Viet Cong stronghold in the Mekong Delta. The photographer labored throughout the war to record what he was witnessing, although none of his photos ever reached the North. A Hanoi press officer recently stated that not only had he never seen any of Khanh's images, he had never heard his name.

VO ANH KHANH

OPPOSITE

South Vietnam, date unknown Members of Artillery Unit X of Battalion 2, Division 4, strike a thoughtful pose after receiving the title of "Hero Unit" for their actions in a liberated zone. Viet Cong units throughout the South carried on a revolutionary program of political assassination and terror intended to destabilize the Saigon government.

VAN PHUONG

Nam Ha Province, 1968 A woman rations out fish sauce to villagers in the North's central coastal region. "It was a hard job for the people who distributed food," says the photographer. "With people suffering from poverty even the slightest unfairness could create trouble." This photo never appeared during the war because it didn't fit the propaganda mold.

MAI NAM

Ca Mau Peninsula, 1970 A guerrilla in the Mekong Delta paddles through a mangrove forest defoliated by Agent Orange. The Americans denuded the landscape with chemicals to deny cover to the Viet Cong. The photographer was sickened by what he saw, since the Vietnamese regard mangrove forests as bountiful areas for agriculture and fishing.

LE MINH TRUONG

THE TRAIL

CHAPTER THREE With the adoption of the Geneva Accords in 1954, Hanoi had been denied unifying the nation, even though peace had been reached with the defeat of the French. In the southern portion of this long, phoenix-like land, Ngo Dinh Diem, a Catholic, usurped power for himself, with the help of Western support. The North licked its wounds, rebuilt, and bided time. But after the fifth Communist Party plenum in 1959, it began to act. The plan for reunification meant first strengthening the southern front. A reconnaissance battalion of trained infiltrators with specialized skills was dispatched to start the process of opening a communication route that would fortify sympathizers in the South. All that existed then were mere dirt tracks; this force would scout out where culverts, cuttings, and way stations could be built.

Initially, the teams only dumped enough stuff at the way stations to keep themselves supplied. The first infiltrators were key cadre, sent to bolster the message of Hanoi's realpolitik among their southern brethren. It would take another year before actual weapons made it down the long trail to the South.

Secret location, 1966
NVA soldiers struggle to build a bridge along the Ho Chi Minh Trail. In 1964, the North began converting existing jungle footpaths into a road system capable of carrying heavy vehicles. Looping several hundred miles from the North through Laos and Cambodia into South Vietnam, the trail would prove pivotal in the war's outcome.

TRAN PHAC

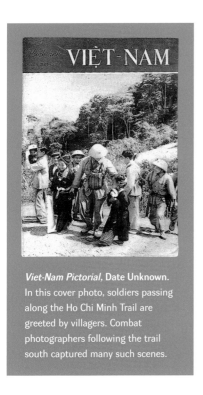

Viet-Nam Pictorial, Date Unknown. In this cover photo, soldiers passing along the Ho Chi Minh Trail are greeted by villagers. Combat photographers following the trail south captured many such scenes.

The first improvements to the trail opened access across the Annam Cordillera via two mountain passes: the more northerly Mu Gia and the Ban Karai near Tchepone in Laos. The southern Laotian towns of Tchepone, Saravan, and Attopu became virtual Vietnamese enclaves. The Laotian panhandle would soon become contested ground, a strategic site for both the North and the South, along with its new ally, the U.S. Hoping to maintain a presence, America was backing royalist Laotian forces. Teams of SOGs (Studies & Operations Groups composed of South Vietnamese and U.S. special forces) were sent to the area to watch and interdict the trail's progress. Many were discovered, captured, or killed, though some did manage to call in air strikes from planes based in Laos, Thailand, Vietnam, and a U.S. Navy task force in the Gulf of Tonkin.

The trail was to prove a difficult target. It was well concealed for a lot of its length, and batteries of antiaircraft artillery fought off incoming strikes. The Vietnamese were past masters at camouflage, a skill honed fighting the French at Dien Bien Phu. Roads cut through the forest and jungle had their passages hidden by overhanging foliage. Most traffic moved by night and initially moved mostly by bicycle. The steel horse, as it came to be known. The French-made Peugeot bike was the preferred steed, though the Czech Favorit became more available as the conflict progressed. One Czech bike held the record, with over a hundred tons of supplies carried down the trail in a single year. The heaviest load recorded was carried by a soldier named Nguyen Dieu, who once hauled 924 pounds on his reinforced Favorit frame.

Photographer Le Minh Truong graduated to the trail having recovered from paralysis caused by a shrapnel hit to the head in Laos in 1956. He was offered a job as a writer-photographer for *Nhan Dan*, the Vietnamese party paper. Among the first to document the primitive passage in 1959 and 1960, he shot Rube Goldberg-like wooden stairs descending a cliff; the *bo doi,* the troops of the Vietnamese Peoples Army, silhouetted in plastic sheeting against the awesome, forest-clad, mist-swirled ridges. He found the trail's wild beauty unsurpassed, he still finds its horrors haunting. The unexpected oblivion of death without warning from a B-52 strike. The camaraderie of working with a small detachment of Pioneer Youth girls, sappers who disarmed ordnance while repairing the damaged trail. He snapped one group of them on and off duty; 24 hours later they all died defusing an unexploded bomb that detonated as they worked.

Truong still speaks with fear of the snakes on the trail. We Western journalists called one variety a "two stepper," as you were dead in two paces when bitten. Then there were the ones that crawled into a troop's hammocks for warmth. Maybe snakebite was a sweeter way to go than the malaria that caused an agonizing 20 percent of Vietnamese casualties. Chinese antimalarial medicines arrived, but never enough. The spectrum of disease defied cure or protection. The weather didn't help, cold and wet in the monsoon season through steamy hot. In the dry season, there was no water—just a new zoo of bugs intent on feeding on any living creature. In places the forest canopy was so thick that a smoke grenade's signal would not penetrate the foliage. Down in that density, men and machines were swallowed alive. Bombing and defoliation pulled back the cover a bit but never enough to enable total interdiction of the network of trails. By 1969 there were 11,500 permanent bo doi, men and women, working round the clock, round the year on the trail network, assisted by bulldozers, graders, rock cutters, and even two steamrollers.

The farther south the trail got, the more exposed it became. Along parts of the Cambodian border, the terrain it passed through was open, studded with sugar palms. Here, it really could be called the "Sihanouk Trail." Prince Sihanouk, in nominally neutral Cambodia, turned a blind eye to the freighters that discharged matériel in the Cambodian seaport of Kompong Som, or "Sihanoukville," where friendly Chinese trucking companies then moved the goodies northeast to the front. These activities were somewhat curtailed when secret U.S. raids over Cambodia began raining down bombs from 1968 on. Still, the border between Vietnam and Cambodia remained porous, the countryside pocked with craters left by the strikes of B-52 bombers. The Saigon River watershed was stripped of foliage by chemical agents—white, blue, and orange—with a half-life akin to that of nuclear waste, 50,000 years. (The area remains toxic to this day. The poisons penetrated the aquifer and continue to show up in fruits and vegetables, causing third- and fourth-generation deformities. This issue is finally being addressed by U.S. authorities through the International Red Cross and the Vietnamese Red Crescent.)

By the mid-1960s, the trail network was the major artery feeding the war in the South and sucking in U.S. troops by the division. The American boys dubbed it the Ho Chi Minh Trail. The Vietnamese called it the Truong Son, after the mountains it threaded through. The French only a decade before had found out how expensive it was to rule these hills, when there had been only a track through them, not the major supply pipeline. Insufficiency of air power had spelled the French downfall. The mist and the rains handed the advantage back to Mr. Charles. Hoping to break the impact of the trail, the U.S. came up with the idea for a technological, multibillion-dollar fence named after the Secretary of Defense, Robert McNamara: It would run from the coast south of the DMZ to Cam Lo in the foothills of the cordillera, a mere 30 miles inland. An array of sensors along the line would trigger an endless stream of aerial firepower from a monitoring base in Thailand. The trail commands, the *binh tram,* countered this by driving herds of cattle down the paths to baffle the seismic devices; chemical detectors—something to do with bugs in cans that could sniff out body smells and so pinpoint live presences—were defeated by hanging buckets of urine in trees. Sound sensors were simply picked up and moved to where they would be useless.

The battle for the trail became an ongoing contest between technology and ingenuity. High tech would not triumph in the end over bamboo or the bicycle. The South and its U.S. allies never succeeded in sealing the 225-mile corridor across the waist of the Annam Cordillera, though efforts were even made to modify the weather—inducing early monsoons by seeding clouds with silver iodide. The weather pattern stayed the same. Another plan was designed to make tracks and river fords impassable by dumping bath oil onto the already muddy route. Should the trail turn to supermud, the binh tram would simply lay down more logs and bamboo matting. Mud was something they understood.

The photographers had to come to grips with mud, too. During the wet, the goo was everywhere, clogging, clinging, debilitating any vehicle, giving even the elephants a hard plod. The weather was an unpredictable enemy. A clear fine day could lead to a

Viet-Nam Pictorial, **1975** A story on the Ho Chi Minh Trail near the end of the war revealed the improved state of the roadway, despite the years-long American bombing campaign. The panorama was shot by Nguyen Dinh Uu.

miserable cold night, with piercing damp. In the jungle nobody could chance lighting a fire just for warmth. The squads of bo doi would hunker down round the small cooking grate that generated enough heat for a communal rice pot. Surprisingly, a jungle does not offer much food. The only Westerners out in this terrain lived on dehydrated rations, at best partially warmed with a heat tab; any water had to be purified.

The onset of the monsoons slowed traffic on the trail to a trickle, but it also restricted plane movements and gave some relief to the binh tram pushing the men and trucks south. Everyone out shooting the trail in those conditions got images redolent of the ooze. Working in the Nam, especially in the central highlands, was always nightmarish. There was something forlorn, spooky about the mist-wreathed hills. The mountains were forbidding, not a zone you could drive around in freely—Indian country. Like our counterparts, we Western shooters would often get stuck in a locale for days, unable to get film or story back to base.

For a photographer, rain and wet is a most loathsome condition. Keeping kit and camera dry and film protected consumes as much ingenuity as making the frames. At least the Vietnamese shooters did not have the complexities of multiple camera bodies and lenses. Practically to a man, they were equipped with East German Prakticas with one fixed, 50mm lens; occasionally, they had another secondhand body but again with a standard lens. Late in the war, they started liberating gear from overrun enemy bases and battlefields. A few took their redoubtable 6x6 Rolleis, (twin lensed, 2-inch, 6mm-square format) to the front. Le Minh Truong, Dinh Dang Dinh, and Tran Cu all used medium-format cameras, and all produced large sparkling negatives, which are now preserved in recycled paper envelopes. It is a marvel to imagine the privation and difficulties they endured to fix those celluloid frames.

The hills always emanated a sense of swallowing you, as if, should you come to grief here, your soul would somehow remain imprisoned in that fetid Hades. Everything rotted, rusted, corroded, was eaten apart by the damp, the bugs, the fungi. Feet turned into peeling sponges; jungle rot crept into pits and body pores; the bugs opened up festering sores; and the water in the streams was a stew of toxic defoliants and jungle-borne fevers. Debilitating dysentery occurred when prudence was not observed. Fevers seemed to hang in the thick of the forest, where there was little ventilation. No breeze stirred the air, so thick it could be cubed with a coup-coup machete, so baking, dusty hot that every step stirred up the microscopic ticks living in the forest litter. Going flat into that stuff when the incoming started meant big red fire ants would penetrate every piece of your well-tucked clothing. Leeches, unerringly scenting blood, dropped from the dripping foliage or crept from the mold and gorged themselves, penetrating into even the eyelets of boots. A boot taken off after a day's yomping through this hostile landscape could decant a cup of your own blood. Trekking in Ho Chi Minh sandals promised the blood-sucking blighters an instant feast. The bo doi and Vietnamese photographers wrapped primitive socks of loose cloth around their feet as a marginal protection. Much later on, with victory on the horizon and better supplies assured, canvas tropical boots would start to come on line.

Camping on the trail was no holiday. At night, at best, you swung fitfully asleep in a hammock, partially protected by a sheet of plastic or a poncho; truck drivers curled

West of Quang Tri, 1970

Vietnamese journalists document the efforts of a team of Youth Volunteers—teenagers from the North—as they use bicycles to ferry rice and weapons along the trail. A trip along the length of the trail took more than a month of hard marching early in the war, but by 1975 some sections had been improved to six-lane roads paralleled by fuel pipelines.

TRONG THANH

Viet-Nam Pictorial, 1972 Documenting the deeds of combat photographers and cameramen, this story told the often harrowing tales behind the images that appeared in Northern periodicals.

up in their cabs. When you made it to a way station, there were rudimentary comforts and, with luck, warm rice. Cold food, cold nights, wandering spooked spirits and the ever present threat of attack disturbed whatever tranquillity might have been achieved.

When you haven't been there, you can't talk about it; when you have, you don't really want to. On meeting an old comrade, a buddy, or even an erstwhile enemy, you often kind of slide over the details nostalgically, a mere suggestion of a situation infilling the insanity and deprivation that had transpired. There is almost a giggle of shared empathy, of having been there and gotten back, alive. The small talk of fellow survivors.

Vuong Khanh Hong, editor and chief photographer of the Truong Son newspaper, spent much of the war with combat engineers and sappers detailed to dispose of unexploded ordnance and to clear post-strike damage. Hong had four boxes of gear in a light truck, his sole equipment to turn out the newspaper with help from the propaganda unit he was attached to. Harassed by the constant bombing, his group would pack up and move on to a new base, dig a bunker for the darkroom, then crank out more prints and prose. The images were hung in the jungle, as Khanh's were in Ca Mau, to boost the morale of the men and women of the binh tram and the transiting bo doi. Hong's unit suffered continual heavy casualties and ill health. In seven years on the trail, Hong had only two trips home to Haiphong. It took him four to five days to get there and the same to get back, ten when the bombing turned bad.

Sitting in his photo shop and studio in Haiphong today, he says his only regret is in not having shot more real photojournalism, records of the horror. He was obliged to toe the politically correct line: The reality of it would not make it to the unit's presses or the outside world. He survived unscathed, though there is a quaver to his voice when recalling those times or showing his few remaining negatives. Many were borrowed by other publications and never seen again, but the bulk of his archives (over 600 negatives) he donated to the Truong Son Museum near Hanoi.

Photographers working the trail were obliged to trust their material, raw film or processed stock plus prints, to a courier service that almost guaranteed its loss. Disastrous strikes on the liberation press headquarters and COSVN (the office controlling both the liberation front and the Viet Cong) in the early '70's obliterated most of their photographic archives. Dinh Dang Dinh lost his whole shoot in a 1974 bombing strike at the south end of the trail.

No film, even when stashed in an ammo box, is bomb safe. The way to keep it safe, as maverick Doan Cong Tinh would prove, was to flout rules, go freelance, and run the pix back personally to the bureau in Hanoi. Tinh would appear, hot film in hand, having broken orders and hitchhiked the trail in record-breaking time, his shots making it to the front pages of the army paper, *Quan Doi Nhan Dan*, three days after he'd taken them.

Surviving was the key for anyone going up or down the trail, and a lot of those who took the trail never returned. The war would consume 2.25 million Vietnamese lives. The wounded were lucky to make it back up the trail in small groups, moving between way stations with medical facilities that were usually thatched, open-sided buildings identical to the storage buildings. These same facilities were used to pass up the various

POWs—Americans, other foreigners, and the countless captives from the southern regime.

By 1970, the trail had become a veritable highway, complete with gas stations. The buried tanks and drums still served up fuel, though their replenishments were now supplemented by a four-inch fuel pipeline that originated in Vinh. A trip down the trail was now available to any photographer or VIP. In 1973, Prince Norodom Sihanouk ascended to Hanoi via the trail in a cavalcade that taxed the binh tram's ability to convert way stations into something deserving of royalty and its retinue.

What was really taking the heat off the trail was the lack of U.S. political will to continue the conflict. Nixon was due to run for reelection in 1972, and the virulent antiwar movement on campuses and city streets was serving to speed up the disengagement timetable. America's heart had been bled of 58,000 men and women, and it wanted out. In country, the remaining GIs were disgruntled, often refusing to go into combat. No one wanted to be the last man killed or left behind. That left the South Vietnamese to fend for themselves on a decapitated budget and a stymied resolve. It became a slide with an ill-defined time frame toward the inevitable.

The North took advantage of the South's weakness, asphalting the trail and adding at least another 240 miles of track. With a good all-weather road, it could start to bring in SAM missiles and countless antiaircraft batteries. The thousands of trucks a week plying the trail were now protected by highly effective defenses.

The trail became a funnel for the Vietnamese photographers. Every agency and paper from Hanoi seemed to have a representative on line to go down. Talking to the survivors today, they say there were probably about 150 different types of bao chi—press and media—who had worked down to the 17th parallel and gotten into the southern Laos panhandle. The Vietnam News Agency set up a forward bureau in the North's panhandle province with a wire machine to transmit both text and photos back to Hanoi. There was an attendant darkroom to accommodate the more liberal supply of film. By now both film and cameras were being liberated as towns and bases were overrun.

Lam Tan Tai documented the new trail runners, skirting through a lunar landscape on roads that could still turn to quagmire, still requiring the brute strength of their drivers and crews to push the supplies through. Now, though, Tran Cu's and Doan Cong Tinh's elephants could plod serenely through the forests again, uninterrupted by gunships. They would soon be back hauling lumber out of the woods.

Today, the Vietnamese, with international backing, are constructing a major highway roughly paralleling the Truong Son trail. About 40 percent complete now, it will eventually cut directly up the spine of the Annam Cordillera, a new inland link between the once warring capitals. Except that Saigon is now Ho Chi Minh City.

Just south of the DMZ, 1972
Photographer Trong Thanh sits on an artillery piece at a U.S. firebase captured by the NVA. The North captured Quang Tri in May during the Eastertide offensive, though the city was essentially destroyed, with most of its inhabitants fleeing south to Hue or Da Nang. Thanh survived the war, only to be killed in Hanoi in 2000 in a lover's spat.

TRONG THANH

113

LE MINH TRUONG

A brush with death brought me to photography. I was born in Hue, fought for the Viet Minh against the French, was "regrouped" to the north in 1954 after Geneva, and remained in the army. Back then my most important mission was being part of the unit that escorted the so-called Laotian "Red Prince" Souphanouvong from North Vietnam to the caves at Sam Nua, the headquarters of the

Pathet Lao liberation movement. Once in Laos, I fought against the CIA-organized troops of Vang Pao. In one early battle in 1956, I was seriously wounded in the head by a piece of flying shrapnel. I thought I was dead. When I woke up I was partially paralyzed, blind, and deaf. But I miraculously recovered my ability to walk, see, and hear. As a wounded soldier, I was unfit to continue in a combat unit and luckily was assigned to be a photographer for the Vietnam News Agency in 1958. From the start, I loved taking photos and traveling around to cover our soldiers.

Perhaps the high point of my career was my pioneering work photographing the Truong Son (Ho Chi Minh) Trail. When I first traveled it in 1959, it was just a jungle track snaking through the mountains, not passable by cars or even bicycles. I recorded our soldiers opening the road with machetes and shovels.

Many people wonder if those early photos I took on the trail were my most difficult. It was not difficult to take the photos, but I did operate under the harsh conditions of living and working in the mountains and forests with few supplies and no comforts. Even back then we were subject to enemy bombing and artillery strikes. There was great danger and much suffering. Still, we did our duty.

I carried film-developing chemicals with me on the difficult journey from Hanoi. In the darkness of the night, along a cool mountain stream, there was plenty of water for the developing, soaking, and washing of the film and prints. In fact, those seemingly hostile mountains provided excellent conditions for developing film. In the Mekong Delta, we were forced to sit under mosquito nets while developing film in the dirty or brackish water so as to avoid being eaten alive by mosquitoes.

Not surprisingly, I like the photos I took along the Truong

Son Trail the best. The scenery was beautiful and the people, whether our soldiers or the local ethnic minorities, were beautiful, too. They displayed the beauty of courage, sacrifice, and endurance against hunger, illness, war, and being so far away from home.

Everyone knew the importance of the trail, that it was the supply lifeline to the South, a key element of the North's victory. The American and Saigon troops tried several times to cut the trail, always unsuccessfully. But we made great sacrifices to defend it. I covered two of those major battles: Khe Sanh in 1968 and southern Laos in 1971. I was also at the battle of Quang Tri in 1972.

Was I afraid? I really didn't think about it, even though many of my friends had been killed. We did our duty just as our frontline soldiers did. Still, I can't help but think that our job was perhaps even more dangerous than that of a soldier. A soldier can shoot just over the rim of the trench he's hiding in. But often a photographer has to jump up and stand on the rim to get a clear shot, making him an easy target.

Kontum, 1972

Le Minh Truong, who became a photographer after being wounded in the 1950s, rests along the trail in the Central Highlands of South Vietnam. During the war against the Americans, he traveled alone, carrying only the gear shown here. To deliver his film back north for publication, he once ran 70 kilometers and swam three rivers along the way.

LE MINH TRUONG

OPPOSITE

Truong Son Mountains, 1966

Finding beauty even in war, the photographer captured this haunting image of troops moving through a canyon along the trail. The Truong Son Mountains form the 750-mile-long spine of Vietnam, stretching along much of the country's western border. To the soldiers of the North, the Ho Chi Minh Trail was known as the Truong Son Road.

LE MINH TRUONG

Hanoi, February 1968 A shot taken through the windshield of a camouflaged truck bound for the Ho Chi Minh Trail shows the Hanoi train station straight ahead. Says the photographer, "I took this because I was leaving for a long time and thought Hanoi might look different when I returned," a reference to the fact that the capital's rail depot was a target of U.S. bombs.

MAI NAM

Quang Binh Province, 1966 NVA troops descend a cliffside stairway just above the DMZ. "At that time we used only small trails on the Vietnamese side of the border," recalls the photographer about the era before the use of trucks. "The eastern part of the trail was very tough. Everyone had to carry at least 20 kilos of equipment in addition to their personal gear."

LE MINH TRUONG

South Vietnam, 1966 Viet Cong guerrillas transport food and ammunition near the southern terminus of the trail. Rivers, streams, and swamps were frequent challenges, along with constant air attacks by U.S. forces, which took an estimated 30,000 lives. The photographer was killed in 1967 during an air raid in Vinh Long Province, in the Mekong Delta.
DINH THUY

OPPOSITE

Tchepone, Laos, March 1971 Laotian guerrillas haul supplies by elephant and foot to NVA troops near Route 9 in southern Laos during South Vietnam's attempted interdiction of the trail. The invasion, Operation Lam Son 719, was intended to test ARVN's ability as U.S. support was winding down. It proved disastrous, with Southern troops fleeing in panic.
DOAN CONG TINH

Ban Don, 1971 NVA soldiers, including the photographer, at right, plan strategy along Route 9 in southern Laos, a major crossroads of the trail, whose numerous routes totaled some 12,000 miles. Despite all efforts to halt the flow, more than 20,000 tons of supplies a month traveled down the trail. U.S. aerial surveillance once revealed 15,000 vehicles on the trail in a single day.

THE DINH

OPPOSITE

Central Vietnam, date unknown Workers repair an elevated jungle pathway. This region underwent devastating air attacks, and nearly all the photographers based here were killed. Early in the war, the North formed Group 559 to build, maintain, and defend the trail. The unit, which grew to 75,000 men and women, claimed to have downed 2,458 U.S. aircraft.

THANH TUNG

Quang Binh, 1969 NVA troops march south through cloud-draped mountains on a section of the Ho Chi Minh Trail near the Vietnam-Laos border. In 1964, the North began improving the trail, begun in 1959, which looped through Laos and Cambodia into South Vietnam. Despite heavy bombing, the one-time series of footpaths was eventually expanded to accommodate heavy trucks and other vehicles.

LE MINH TRUONG

LAM TAN TAI

1965 was the year of escalation. I had just graduated in archaeology from the University of Hanoi after having spent four years studying in Moscow. I was drafted and ordered to go south down the Ho Chi Minh Trail. For us southerners, it was a great honor and opportunity to be selected to go south, especially as a photographer. Only the most physically fit were chosen. We were motivated

not only by patriotism but also by a youthful spirit of adventure. We had a saying "Nhut Xanh Co, Nhi Do Nguc," green grass or a red chest, meaning if we died the grass would grow greener and if we lived our chests would be covered with red medals. And despite the obvious dangers I had always wanted to return to my birthplace in Dong Thap province in the Mekong Delta.

My constant companion was my small East German-made camera that I bought in Moscow, where I fell in love with photography. From the moment we jumped off the trucks in Quang Binh Province, just north of the Demilitarized Zone, I clicked that camera nonstop for four long months as we walked down the trail to the far south. I had such energy. Most of the time I would run uphill ahead of the supply convoys or climb up hillsides to get better angles of the trucks and men winding through the mountain passes and crossing bridges.

The farther south we went and the greater the difficulties became, the less energy I had to get that special angle to make a great picture. The death and destruction slowed me down the most. A very close friend, a young woman who was heading south to become a teacher in our resistance zone, was seriously wounded in one of the frequent B-52 strikes and was evacuated back to the North. I saw many young soldiers die from dysentery because they drank water directly from mountain streams without boiling it. Many others died from malaria simply because they were too tired to hang their mosquito nets over their hammocks at night. Luckily, I was only sick with malaria fever once.

The mud and the heavy loads we carried, including seven kilos of rice, which had to last for two weeks, also sapped our strength. We supplemented our meager rice supplies by foraging for edible plants and fruits in the forest.

We walked all day and sometimes at night, with only one day's rest a week. That's when I'd process my film. Just after eating at dusk, I'd prepare my developing solutions. Then, around 9 p.m., when everyone was asleep, I'd develop the week's film. The vast dark forest was my giant darkroom. In the morning I'd rinse the prints in a stream and then hang them from trees to dry. In the afternoon I'd cut them to size and do the captions. I'd wrap the prints and negatives in paper and put them in a plastic bag, which I kept close to my body. That way the photos would stay dry and could be easily found if I got killed.

My destination was Cu Chi, just north of Saigon, near the base of the U.S. 25th Infantry Division. We lived in the tree lines on the edge of villages that had been occupied by the enemy. We had no tunnels, like the now famous Cu Chi tunnels, to hide in. We buried large water jars in the ground, leaving only the mouth exposed. When villagers alerted us that the enemy was coming, each man would jump into a jar and cover it with a camouflaged lid, leaving only a tiny opening through which to breathe. If the enemy came too close, we'd have to close the lid tightly. At least two of my comrades suffocated that way while they waited for the enemy to move on.

My closest brush with death was during the 1968 Tet offensive. We had infiltrated Saigon and were filming our forces as they fought in Cholon. But the reinforcements we were expecting never came and we were trapped. Two of my friends, a film cameraman and a reporter, were killed. I lost an eye to an exploding M-79 grenade but was rescued by two older women who supported the resistance. They rushed me to a public hospital where I checked in as a wounded civilian, thanks to the fake Saigon government identity card I had used to sneak into the city.

Truong Son Mountains, July 1974
NVA soldiers work together to push their Russian-made truck out of the mud. Frequent quagmires along the trail could limit a day's progress to little more than a mile. Even after the trail was improved to support trucks and tanks, a steady line of human bearers trudged along, carrying packs sometimes equal to their own body weight.

LAM TAN TAI

Cam Lo, June 1972 A village elder fans a sleeping driver at a stop on the DMZ, a show of how locals did whatever they could to support the war. Trucks often moved down the trail at night to avoid detection, although even during daylight the traffic continued. Knowing that bombing attacks often occurred at the same times of day allowed drivers to take cover.

HOANG KIM DANG

Unknown location, July 1974 Trucks roar along a muddy part of the trail where the roadway had been widened. Phone lines were strung along the trail so convoys could communicate without resorting to radios, which could be monitored. Support facilities, mostly underground, included hospitals, fuel storage tanks, and supply caches.

LAM TAN TAI

Ha Tinh Province, 1967

Youth Volunteer La Thi Tam counts bombs falling near Dong Loc village, a main junction on the trail that was frequently attacked. Delayed-fuse bombs buried themselves in the ground and detonated under the weight of traffic. The falling bombs were counted so those that didn't explode on impact could be located and deactivated.

VAN BAO

OPPOSITE

North Vietnam, date unknown

Local militia and villagers camouflage a bridge with brush and banana leaves to hide it from American bombers. The bridge was not identified when the image was made to keep its location a secret during wartime. Masters of the art of camouflage, the Vietnamese were often able to thwart the most sophisticated aerial surveillance.

PHOTOGRAPHER UNKNOWN

Quang Binh Province, 1967 The lurid glare of napalm engulfs a section of the trail. One of the war's most feared weapons, napalm could suffocate its victims even without contact. The photographer was at grave risk to make this image. "We worked with rudimentary equipment, no zoom lenses like nowadays, so we had to get close to the subject."

LE MINH TRUONG

Quang Binh Province, March 1969 A six-negative panorama shows
supply trucks rolling through a ghost forest denuded by defoliants
dropped by American planes. The principal U.S. defoliant was Agent
Orange, 40 million pounds of which were sprayed over five million
acres, creating environmental havoc. Agent Orange-related birth
defects still occur in Vietnam.

VAN SAC

Cu Chi, 1975 Youth volunteers clear land to build a new army base outside Cu Chi at the trail's southern terminus, just 25 miles northeast of Saigon. The site of extensive underground tunnels that were a target of American operations throughout the war, Cu Chi would be a staging area for the final assault on the Southern capital.

MAI NAM

OPPOSITE

Location unknown, 1969 NVA soldiers rest in hammocks a few hundred meters off the trail, where they were less exposed to U.S. warplanes. "Young people going to the South went with a sense of devotion," says the photographer. "The bombing of the North ignited them to go fight. I was like these other young people. I went with that same passion."

LE MINH TRUONG

Location unknown, 1970 A Youth Volunteer plays her guitar during a rest break along the trail. Assigned to a team of young women who deactivated delayed-fuse bombs dropped by U.S. planes, the teenager was killed the day after this image was made. "There was nothing left," recalls the photographer, "not even flesh. Nothing except pieces of clothing scattered about."

LE MINH TRUONG

Location and date unknown Viet Cong guerrilla Bui Van Quang carries a wounded friend during action along the trail on the Cambodian border. Bui bore his comrade for two hours while under attack. Although the Viet Cong led the resistance early in the war, after 1968's Tet offensive, North Vietnamese troops did most of the fighting in the South.

PHOTOGRAPHER UNKNOWN

Ha Tinh Province, date unknown A government delegation meets with soldiers and militia in the village of Dong Loc, a trail crossroads in southern North Vietnam and today a revered spot for Vietnamese tourists. This three-negative panorama conveyed the popular support of the war in the North and the close association of the government with the people.

PHOTOGRAPHER UNKNOWN

Can Le, June 30, 1966 NVA forces cross a river on a section of the trail near the Cambodian border. French President Charles de Gaulle visited Cambodia in September 1966, urging American withdrawal from Vietnam, but by year's end, U.S. troop strength had reached nearly 400,000. The North, meanwhile, continued to infiltrate thousands of troops monthly.

LE CHI HAI

OPPOSITE

Quang Tri Province, 1972 An NVA propaganda unit passes through a village near the DMZ. Their loudspeakers were used to urge southern villagers to support the liberation effort. In 1974 the photographer was documenting the trail near Loc Ninh, just north of Saigon, when bombs destroyed his cameras and nearly 100 rolls of film. "In an instant I lost all my work."

DINH DANG DINH

Cambodia, 1972 Guerrilla forces march inside the Cambodian border across from Tay Ninh, a Viet Cong stronghold. Movement through open areas such as this was dangerous, although marginally safer in Cambodia and Laos. Cambodia did come under air attack in the 1969 "secret" bombings, and U.S.-ARVN troops briefly crossed the border in 1970.

LE MINH TRUONG

Southern Laos, April 1971 NVA soldiers dash past ARVN dead near the "Hill Without a Name." The fierce fighting occurred during Operation Lam Son 719, the South's failed attempt to interdict the trail—a defeat that foretold the war's outcome. Recalling the intense days of combat, the photographer said, "When I came back to the old battlefields I cried so hard."

DOAN CONG TINH

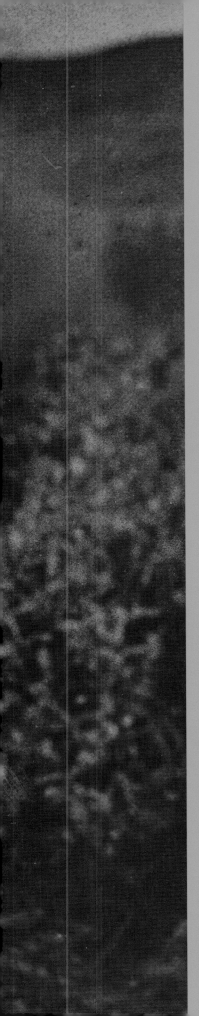

QUYET THANG: RESOLVE TO WIN

CHAPTER FOUR

The world woke up on January 31, 1968, to a new kind of live—or almost live—event played out on global television: A squad of Viet Cong sappers blowing a hole in the wall surrounding the U.S. Embassy in downtown Saigon, then holding the embassy grounds until killed. The audacious attack, minutes away from the Western media corps's offices, heralded a simultaneous assault and overrunning of nearly every major district and provincial town across the South. The Tet offensive, begun on the Lunar New Year that ushered in the Year of the Monkey, was on, covered by hundreds of media representatives from every continent. Their coverage gave us a wealth of iconic frames and footage.

The North Vietnamese had gotten their photojournalists into position as well. Though always reluctant to endanger the bao chi, the media—key holders of information the enemy would love to obtain—the North knew that press images and reports of the offensive were needed. So this time it was willing to take a gamble with the press. Still, most of the photographers were assigned to rearguard units designated to follow up after objectives were achieved.

Quang Tri Province, 1970
An NVA soldier aids a wounded comrade while under fire just south of the DMZ. Like many of his fellow war photographers, Doan Cong Tinh had to personally carry his film back north for publication. "We did not have the means that the American photographers had. We had to deliver our babies ourselves."
DOAN CONG TINH

151

Viet-Nam Pictorial, **1972** The epic battle of Quang Tri garnered significant coverage, but photographs inside the ancient citadel were hard to obtain. Doan Cong Tinh's image at right provided a rare glimpse.

The North had hoped that the Tet offensive would inspire a general uprising in the South. Within a few days, though, Southern and U.S. forces had reorganized and inflicted heavy casualties. In May, the North tried again, mounting the mini-Tet offensive and once again taking large tracts of Saigon. A virtual outbreak of peace ensued that summer, as various diplomats struggled to agree to the shape of a permanent peace at the Paris talks. During the lull, the Vietnamese replaced infrastructure and men and matériel. Not surprisingly, there are few images from this period, as the media on both sides had taken heavy hits.

Tet had been a long time coming, the planning and provisioning taking years. In the end, while it left a wound that took much binding, its psychological effects signaled the beginning of the end. America's chief pundit, CBS's Walter Cronkite, reported from the ancient capital of Hue, just below the DMZ, that he now doubted an American victory. A global public doubted, too. The attacks had brought home to the U.S. and South Vietnam the inevitability of the outcome of the war and the impossibility of policing an entire country rife with enemy sympathizers—or of defeating an enemy with the resolve to come back again and again.

Uncle Ho had fostered the determination to win, the dream of nationhood that had been an ancestral ideal for the Vietnamese. The pattern had been created as far back as A.D. 40, when the fabled Trung Sisters had driven the Chinese out. Now Ho and his generals were melding that ancient revolutionary tradition with modern technology and ideals. No sacrifice was too great for the cause. The resolve to win, *"Quyet Thang,"* had been instilled. Victory would be achieved.

In the colonial era, the French had attempted to infiltrate all aspects of Vietnamese life, to restructure the society and culture. They had failed. The Vietnamese had developed a resolve that occasionally ebbed though never waned—tradition upheld as a wise thread through life, diligence and learning championed.

Ho had been educated in French schools, but on a deeper level he was steeped in the mandarin traditions of Taoism, Confucianism, and Buddhism—the triple threads in the Vietnamese tapestry of belief. He brought those beliefs to his understanding of communism, shaping it into something uniquely Vietnamese. Stirring in Russian and Chinese doctrines, he absorbed what he believed to be of use. The rest was let go, often rejected outright. This brand of socialism, of communism, became the central tenet of Vietnamese political and official life.

During the course of the war, photography became a prime medium for inspiring commitment to the cause. The older photographers who joined Ho's fight tended to be revolutionaries first, struggling for the nationalist cause, and Communist Party members second. We tend to paint all of them red, whereas we should see them primarily as activists holding a line, obliged to sign on to the party for the proverbial card. They were unquestionably part of the trusted hard core, essential to the North's propaganda machine and to the war effort.

Nguyen Dinh Uu, Dinh Dang Dinh, and Tran Cu did justice to civilian and military activities, and the glorious frames they shot during the battle against the French at Dien Bien Phu were replayed on newspaper pages and in *Viet-Nam Pictorial,* particularly when

Ca Mau Peninsula, 1968
Guerrillas in the Mekong Delta study a map as they prepare for the Tet offensive that came days later. Attacking cities throughout the South, Viet Cong and NVA forces lost an estimated 40,000 men, though they achieved a psychological victory. According to the photographer, several of the people shown here were killed.

VO ANH KHANH

there was a low point in the struggle. Photography used as pure propaganda, exhorting the people to steel themselves for another battle, another round of fighting.

Beyond propaganda, the photographers were critical to intelligence gathering. Dinh Dang Dinh and others worked in recon units as scouts; some photographers even started first as scouts, before they ever picked up a camera. Back then, in those early days, the North was fighting against the odds. After Tet, it grew bolder, even as the bombing grew fiercer. Death became accepted as something that could befall anyone anytime. Still, the resolve to continue the struggle focused the Northern fighters and photographers away from the probable.

Viet-Nam Pictorial, which had been publishing in a number of languages, cut back to Vietnamese and English. International distribution was always a problem for the North. The Vietnam News Agency relied on a network of agents, distributing out of its embassies

Viet-Nam Pictorial, **1967** Guerrilla forces challenge an ARVN unit in the swamps of South Vietnam. Images taken in the South by Viet Cong photographers often failed to reach the offices of Northern publications.

in the Eastern bloc and other European countries to the sympathetic local press. It could take up to a week for a set of prints with a story appended to reach a foreign desk, and by then it was out of date, overtaken by other hot media events and breaking news. Not until late '71, when Hanoi at last got itself a decent wire-photo system, was the problem alleviated.

In the meantime, the North copiously submitted its films and photographs to festivals and shows in socialist and nonaligned nations. It consistently won prizes, and not just for its correct revolutionary ardor and heroic content. The style and form of the material was always strong, and it should have seen more exposure in the non-communist world. The West never really saw the sufferings of the Vietnamese, their joys or woes, their agonies and ecstasies. Everyday life in the North or at the front was only glimpsed through occasional visits by a handful of trusted Western photographers and writers.

As the war wore on, a new generation of photographers began to emerge, well founded in the polemics of the party but devoted to the art of journalism and photography. This new breed of photojournalists were risktakers, content to incur the wrath of the system in their zeal to get the picture. Doan Cong Tinh was one of them. He perfected his coverage by staying close to one squad of fighters, moving with a local guide, defying orders, using the ultimate photographer's tools of ingenuity and guile. He proved equally adept in the open country, taking shots of firebases along the old McNamara Line or deep in the forest.

The other skill he acquired in the '71 offensives, a truly fear-conquering one, was street fighting. By then towns in the South were city size, swollen with refugees. Any urban warfare is extremely dangerous; fire can emanate from indistinguishable places, the direction of the sound obscured by buildings. Life and action are conducted in short bursts, from cover to cover, trying to snap or shoot on the run to the next doorway, wall, rubble pile, or wrecked vehicle. It is a dreamscape for the sniper lying in ambush, should you be the target. It's the hardest scenario to predict, timing of any move the key to survival. Overlay that with continuous incoming artillery and naval fire, lay on chopper gunships and fighter bombers, and you have a glimpse of what street fighting is like, familiar now from Sarajevo to Groznyy.

Maybe it's what prepared Doan Cong Tinh for the battle at Quang Tri, a classic 18th-century citadel of bricked ramparts, redoubts, and a central command bastion. Beyond that were town combat complexes and several strategic bridges. Like Hue, Quang Tri was within range of offshore naval gunfire. When the North hit it in 1972, their firepower came accompanied by armor, battalions of heavy tanks and a fearsome quantity of long-range artillery and APC (armored personnel carriers) with shock troops.

The battled raged for three days, and Doan Cong Tinh went into the heat of it, against orders. He worried that his portfolio of this urban nightmare would get him expelled from the Communist Party. It didn't. Both he and the North emerged from the Quang Tri inferno victorious.

With the North gaining ground, more equipment also started to come available, liberated down South, then diligently recorded and sent to the rear for use by an impoverished but talented fraternity of comrades. One of that lucky fraternity, Trong Thanh, got his hands on a Leica M, supplementing his two Prakticas. He remembered it with the joy any photographer would have on first touching, holding, and squeezing off a frame on this masterpiece. Thanh would get in close, his images compassionate. In one incident, he was in an attack on a South Vietnamese naval vessel that went horribly wrong. The North's forces opened fire too soon, enemy helicopter gunships spotted them and tore them up. Under fire, Trong Thanh evacuated a comrade with a sucking chest wound away from the firefight, transporting him on an improvised raft across a lagoon. He had to ditch the Leica and most of his gear. His comrade died in his arms, sobbing for his mother.

The North's unflinching resolve to win the war waned momentarily in September 1969, with Ho's death of heart failure at the age of 79. The nation was shaken to the core, war stopped nearly everywhere. Such was the common respect felt for their sage. The system he had orchestrated, the party mechanism that had been built up over three decades, did manage to keep rolling, if bowed by grief. The instilled will, the determination, lapped the North through the crisis.

Twenty plus photographers documented Ho's state funeral, attended by a panoply of the communist leadership. For a week the press was full of little but eulogies for the lost leader. *Nhan Dan,* the party paper, and *Viet-Nam Pictorial* both ran special issues on the funeral.

After Ho's loss, the war continued with the same resolve. The opposition was now withdrawing troops and units at a pace commensurate with the degree of Vietnamization of ARVN forces going on in the South. Desertion and AWOL lists were escalating there even as units were being levied, equipped, and trained. The brunt of the casualties were now being borne by South Vietnamese troops, as Americans tried not to be the last ones out in a body bag. The South's corrupt government profited even further from a populace that had been terrified into moving into the cities. Security evaporated, and the roads out of cities became no go. Back in the U.S., the determination to pursue the war had gone. The battle of wills had passed.

As the pendulum swung in the North's favor, Hanoi stopped trying so hard to protect its photographers and their film from enemy intelligence. More were killed and wounded regularly but even this did not dampen the new buoyant mood embracing everyone. At least now the remains of the dead were often recoverable.

Of the survivors, few escaped scratch free. All of them, like the veterans of the Western press, still live with recurrent hearing and back problems. Anyone who has ever been near a bomb or shell explosion has suffered residual effects just from the concussion. Everyone who lived through the war recalls the terror of being blitzed in tunnels, bunkers, and shelters. The nightmare of interment in a collapsed earthwork, the terrifying whistle of an incoming shell or a bomb does not dissipate easily from the psyche.

Take the Unification Express train south from Hanoi today, and just north of the city of Thanh Hoa you will see on the southern bluffs above the Ma River 36-foot-high letters emblazoned in white. Quyet Thang—Resolve to Win. It is the same message, the same vision that the fighter and bomber pilots during the war would have seen as they screamed overhead. Only in the last few years has Thanh Hoa itself begun to resemble a normal city. Remainders of the war linger still, like the letters on the cliff.

Mekong Delta, 1973
A Viet Cong guerrilla is treated by a medical team along a branch of the Mekong River. Makeshift medical facilities were necessary for constantly moving guerrilla forces throughout the South, although underground field hospitals along the Ho Chi Minh Trail were equipped with sanitary operating rooms.
LE MINH TRUONG

DOAN CONG TINH

Getting to the front was the big thing. It was never easy. Many of my colleagues never arrived at the scene of the action; they were killed along the way. I witnessed two of my best friends die. Both have streets named after them: Nghia Dung in Hanoi and Bui Dinh Tuy in Saigon. But tragedy for some led to my success, first during Saigon's Lam Son 719 operation in 1971, when

its army launched an attack into Laos in a foolish attempt to cut the Ho Chi Minh Trail, and then again during our heroic capture and defense of Quang Tri Province and its citadel in 1972. Both times, I was one of the lucky few who was in the right place at the right time and thus was able to take many exclusive photos that were published in Hanoi's newspapers.

Quang Tri was the deadliest ground. Not counting the thousands of bombs falling from the sky, American and Saigon troops were pouring 20,000 artillery shells a day into the citadel at Quang Tri that we had just liberated in May 1972. The Americans didn't want to leave one brick standing on another. Airplanes also poured from the sky yellow strips of toxic chemicals that seemed to spread out and envelop the citadel in a tent of deadly yellow poison. With such destruction raining down, I had to get inside the citadel to document what was happening, because the whole country wanted to know how our soldiers were holding up under the stress. I had come down to Quang Tri from the North with a tank unit that got me close to the battle. Along the way, I picked up the nickname "the Flag," because I was so visible, constantly riding on the outside of the tanks and standing up and snapping pictures, even when we were under air attack. I managed to sneak into the citadel for a quick visit in May, just before the enemy's counterattack started.

Getting back into the old fortress was not easy. So heavy was the bombing and shelling that it was too dangerous for the tank unit I was with to proceed. And besides the physical danger, our authorities had banned reporters and photographers from traveling to the citadel. Yet I was determined to go. I pleaded my case with the Communist Party chief of a village that was located on the north side of the Thach Han River,

just across from the citadel. He refused. I could understand why. Standing on the riverbank, I could see nothing but deep and wide bomb craters and fallen trees on the other side. Then, underneath my feet, I heard voices coming from our underground bunkers. So I went to look for the tunnel entrance, where I found some soldiers. When I asked them how I could get into the citadel, they told me that it was impossible, but I could photograph the wounded being brought out on a nearby evacuation route. Those were not the pictures I wanted. Rather, I wanted photos of our combat troops living and fighting in the citadel, pictures like the ones I had taken just weeks before at the start of our offensive. In one, our soldiers were planting a victory flag on one of the first firebases we had captured from Saigon's army; in another, our soldiers are pointing and laughing at the words "King of the War," written on the gun turret of a Saigon tank they had just captured.

One day, as I pressed my case with the party official, two female guerrillas were listening and one jokingly said: "If this obstinate reporter wants to go into the citadel, we'll take him." The women, both liaison officers who frequently carried messages in and out of the citadel, bravely volunteered to be my guides. With that, the party official finally gave me permission to go. But that night as we approached the Thach Han River on our way to the citadel, the women warned me how dangerous the journey was. "Shrapnel falls like rain on the river that is illuminated like daylight by dropping flares," they said. "We could easily be killed." Still, we managed to cross it and arrive safely in the citadel. On my first trip, the city hall inside the citadel was still intact. On this, my second trip, it and everything else were in ruins. Only the smiles of our soldiers inside remained the same. One said to

Hanoi, 1972 Doan Cong Tinh, far right, stands with his pregnant wife and her family before leaving to cover the Easter offensive in Quang Tri. Traditionally, a Vietnamese father names a child before birth, but Tinh didn't dare to because he wasn't sure if he'd survive. "Although fearing the worst for me," he says of his wife, "she didn't cry."

DOAN CONG TINH

me, "Tomorrow some of us may not be here, but the citadel will live forever in the history of our country."

A year earlier, during Saigon's disastrous Lam Son 719 operation, I was lucky enough to hook up with a combat unit reinforcing our liberation troops that had just captured Hill 456, a Saigon firebase overlooking the Ho Chi Minh Trail inside southern Laos. In front of my eyes was the terrible scene of Saigon's defeat. I walked through a battlefield littered with smoldering tanks, armored vehicles, downed helicopters, all sorts of American weaponry, and the bodies of dead and dying Saigon airborne troops. While I was frantically snapping away, enemy artillery started falling and aircraft roared overhead. Yet even as two jets

swooped low to drop bombs, our troops kept moving through this curtain of fire and smoke. I took cover for a moment, then rushed back to continue photographing the shadowy figures of our liberation soldiers moving through the smoke-filled field, which was strewn with dead bodies lying frozen in all kinds of contorted positions. The battle lasted for three more days. During that time, an entire Saigon tank unit was destroyed, scores of armored vehicles were captured and dozens more burned out by B-40 rocket fire, and at least 400 Saigon soldiers were killed. I took photos of all that and even of our soldiers jumping on enemy tanks, killing or capturing the drivers and crew, then using the captured vehicles to attack other enemy targets. After the battle, one senior officer took my hand and said with a smile: "Business must have been good for you guys. So good that I'm afraid you may not have had enough film to capture all the images we made for you."

But taking the pictures was only part of our duty. Most of us had to hand-carry our work back home—on foot. When I left the citadel or the front in southern Laos, I felt a heavy responsibility to bring those photos—the documentary evidence of our struggle for independence and unification—as quickly as possible back to Hanoi. As I went, I always carried with me a last will and testament of sorts that I had scribbled on a piece of paper

and rolled into my precious bundle of exposed film. My message read: "If I am killed or wounded, please urgently deliver this film to the army newspaper, *Quan Doi Nhan Dan,* 7 Pham Dinh Phung St., Hanoi."

After I left the southern Laos front, I ran for seven days and nights, almost nonstop, neglecting food and sleep, to get my film back up the trail to Hanoi. I hitchhiked and begged for rides on our supply convoys. To get a ride, I sometimes had to bribe the truck drivers by offering up my most prized possessions, like my watch or money or food rations. I even gave one driver a precious bicycle I had come by. No matter how desperate I was at times, I was not going to give my film to a military courier who could lose it or sell it or be blown up with it.

I wasn't a war photographer for a very long time, just from 1970 to 1973. My time at the front was not long, because we spent most of our time either getting there or delivering the film back up the trail to Hanoi. Strangely, I think I always wanted to be a combat photographer. I volunteered for the army when I was 19, and I graduated as an artillery officer from our military academy in 1965. While I was at school, I bought a Russian-made Feddeka from a classmate for 30 dong. I couldn't afford it, as my student salary was only five-dong a-month, so my father and brother each chipped in 15 dong and bought it for me. I taught myself to take pictures and started developing stamp-size photos with a flashlight. In 1967 I was serving as a political officer in a military region. As part of my propaganda job, I wrote articles for the army paper, but my commander saw that my main interest was photography, and he issued me an East German Practika. Soon the paper needed another photographer to cover the southern front. I volunteered immediately. I had always longed to be in combat situations, to be part of the war effort, to do my duty to defend and unify our divided country.

I easily could have avoided combat, thanks to my father's high connections. Some of his best friends were senior officials with ministerial rank. Most families enjoying such high connections sent their sons to study overseas in order to avoid the draft. But even though I was a COCC, or *con ong chau cha* (a son of the powerful), there was never any question of my not going to the front. And I'm proud of my family's correct stand that I should serve the country. I may have been a photographer, but once at the front I was also a soldier. My camera was my weapon, just as a gun is a soldier's. We photographers had to have the same courage as our soldiers.

Soc Trang, 1973 A Viet Cong guerrilla stands guard in the Mekong Delta. "You could find women like her almost everywhere during the war," says the photographer. "She was only 24 years old but had been widowed twice. Both her husbands were soldiers. I saw her as the embodiment of the ideal guerrilla woman, who'd made great sacrifices for her country."

LE MINH TRUONG

Nghe An Province, 1966 Ethnic Hmong guerrillas skirmish outside Nam Cam village in the mountains of south-central North Vietnam. Recruited by all sides in the war, even by the CIA, these Laotian tribal people were excellent fighters and used whatever weapons they had, such as the bows and arrows carried by the lead soldier in this photo.

NGUYEN DINH UU

OPPOSITE

Vietnam-Cambodia border, 1972 Guerrillas guard an outpost protected by poisoned bamboo punji stakes. Sharpened then hardened with fire, punji stakes were often hidden where enemy soldiers would step on them. Such booby traps were meant to wound, not kill, because wounded soldiers slowed down their unit, and medevacs gave away its position.

LE MINH TRUONG

Dong Thap Muoi, 1973 A Viet Cong unit moves warily through defoliated swampland in the Plain of Reeds. Such difficult terrain—soft, muddy, and exposed to enemy fire—often meant guerrillas could travel only a few kilometers per day. "Was I afraid?" mused the photographer about dangerous situations like this. "I really didn't think about it."

LE MINH TRUONG

Dong Thap Muoi, date unknown Approaching by boat, Viet Cong guerrillas and local farmers surround ARVN soldiers in the swampy Plain of Reeds. This "accidental" panorama consists of two of six frames of a live combat scene. They were made with a Rolleiflex portrait camera, a large, awkward model not often used to take war photos.

MAI LOC

Phung Hiep District, 1969 Local guerrillas engage the enemy near Can Tho, the Mekong Delta's commercial center. An injured Viet Cong lies at right, and the enemy is straight ahead, beyond the trees. Inhabited mainly by ethnic Vietnamese, with many Cambodians in the southwest, the 26,000-square-mile delta was fertile ground for revolution.

LY WAY

Can Tho, 1974 Viet Cong guerrillas from the Tay Do Division attack the Thuan Nhon base. The photographer's wife, who was with him when he made this night photo, explained that a flash didn't attract attention during an operation against American/ARVN forces, since there were so many phosphorous flares and other visual distractions.

LY WAY

Cai Nuoc, 1973 A female guerrilla in the Mekong Delta takes a captured ARVN soldier to an unknown fate. The Viet Cong were respected fighters. Outnumbered ten to one at the Battle of Ap Bac, in 1963, they still managed to impose a stinging defeat on ARVN forces. At that time, the VC controlled more villages than did the Saigon government.

VO ANH KHANH

OPPOSITE

Ca Mau Peninsula, 1972 An ARVN soldier surrenders to a Viet Cong guerrilla. "The soldier had hid in the brush below an ARVN camp that had been taken over the night before," explains the photographer, "and they found him in the morning, terrified." Although well-equipped, ARVN units were often led by incompetent officers, and troops suffered low morale.

VO ANH KHANH

South Vietnam, date unknown Viet Cong meet the enemy face-to-face, most likely in the Mekong Delta or Plain of Reeds. This image is unique in that it shows both sides engaged in combat, ARVN soldiers at the top and Viet Cong in the foreground. The VC have outflanked the enemy at left and right, which likely meant the ARVN unit was wiped out.

HOANG MAI

South Vietnam, date unknown Nurse Pham Thi Kim Lien tends a
wounded comrade at a trench fortification. Though the Viet Cong
could be a shadowy force, striking then quickly disappearing, at times
they dug in against the enemy in "liberated zones," most often rural
villages where discontent with the Saigon government was high.

PHOTOGRAPHER UNKNOWN

Tay Ninh, 1967 An injured ARVN soldier captured at Duc Hue rests at Prison Camp #12, near the Vietnam-Cambodia border. Often unable to care for POWs, the Viet Cong commonly took no prisoners. The city of Tay Ninh, part of the communists' Iron Triangle stronghold, was a jumping-off point for insurgents seeking sanctuary in Cambodia.

LAM TAN TAI

U Minh Forest, September 15, 1970 A victim of American bombing, ethnic Cambodian guerrilla Danh Son Huol is carried to an improvised operating room in a mangrove swamp in this Viet Cong haven on the Ca Mau Peninsula. This scene was an actual medical situation, not a publicity set up. The photographer, however, considered the image unexceptional and never printed it.

VO ANH KHANH

South Vietnam, date unknown. A Viet Cong puppet troupe performs
along the Vietnam-Cambodia border. Soldier Huynh Minh Sieng,
seated second from right, joins the troupe for a portrait. Equivalent to
Bob Hope revues, these simple entertainments were important to the
Viet Cong and to Northerners serving far from home.

TRAN NHU

Song Gianh, 1969 Performers from the Song Gianh Art Troupe entertain
an artillery unit just north of the DMZ. Such shows were designed to
cheer up and rally the troops.

PHOTOGRAPHER UNKNOWN

VO ANH KHANH

I worked largely in the U Minh Forest, our extensive liberated zone of marsh and mangroves and villages in the southern Mekong Delta, not far from where I was born. We were always under attack by American and Saigon forces. But in the late 1960s and early 1970s, the enemy was able to concentrate its firepower on us. The Americans called it the "U Minh Forest Weeding

Campaign." Their aim was criminal. To annihilate our liberation forces there, the Americans decided to destroy the U Minh and everything in it: our homes, fields, livestock, and field hospitals. They sprayed Agent Orange from planes and river patrol boats to defoliate the vast expanse of mangrove forests, bamboo, and coconut trees in which our people and fighters lived. They fired artillery nonstop. Large planes and helicopters rained down machine-gun bullets on anything that moved. B-52s and fighter aircraft bombed us day and night. The sweep of destruction was so vast that much of the landscape looked like the end of the world: Nothing but leafless and broken trees and the burned and broken remains of houses. I tried to capture all this devastation and our resistance to it on film. Our people and the world had to know what the U.S. was doing, and how we were fighting back to save our country.

To do so, I had to react quickly to the first sound of planes coming and to fresh reports of new attacks. It wasn't easy. I usually traveled with a guerrilla unit. We had to move silently through the swamps and the mud with our trouser legs rolled up. Mosquitoes and leeches were a constant nuisance. Usually we went barefoot to keep from slipping or getting bogged down in the mire. On narrow, muddy trails, our toes had to grip the ooze like claws. To cross a monkey bridge—a construction of thin bamboo poles over a canal—our feet had to be as limber as hands. In the dry season, when the water level was low, I frequently had to jump out of the little sampan we traveled in and push it through the mud. Often, I had to climb trees to look out for the enemy and to get a better angle to photograph the destruction. One misstep at any time along the way and my camera and film would have been ruined. Dropping a camera, or allowing it to

get wet, was even worse than a soldier losing his weapon. There were no replacements.

One evening in early 1971, as a film crew and I were walking with a guerrilla squad to Khanh Lam village, where we planned to spend the night, I heard the sound of planes coming. We immediately took cover in a dense stand of tall reeds near a hamlet that had already been razed. Only a handful of thatched huts remained standing under a few barren trees. Suddenly a twin-rotor Chinook helicopter appeared above some coconut palms whose tops had been sheared off by enemy fire. It began slowly circling over the village and us like a hunting dog sniffing out its prey. It was so close I could clearly see a helmeted American soldier leaning out the door and aiming his powerful machine gun in our direction.

Then the chopper seemed to find what it had been looking for: a well-camouflaged dirt-and-wood shelter sitting between

two clumps of banana trees. To grab its prey, the chopper began flying in tight circles and quickly dropping in altitude. Then suddenly the chopper began pouring out a great rain of machine-gun fire and dropping hand grenades on the target. The explosions kicked up a blinding dust, dirt, fire, and smoke storm and gave off a nauseating, burning smell. My gut hurt as if the explosions were happening inside me.

We couldn't bear to stay hidden and allow the destruction to continue. Two guerrillas lying next to me began shooting their AK-47s at the chopper hovering just in front of us. At the same time, I stood up and started taking pictures. The chopper shot back and, momentarily, the chopper's and our fire crossed paths as if we were in a deafening duel. I think the guerrilla fire must have hit the chopper, which suddenly gained altitude and flew away. We quickly ran toward the bunker through the smoke and dust clouds, hoping that nothing terrible had

happened. But the top of the shelter had been blown away, one corner had collapsed, and the banana trees that had served as camouflage were leafless and shredded. The place looked as if a bulldozer had flattened it. We immediately began digging with our hands. Incredibly, we found people alive, buried deep in the dirt. We pulled out 17 survivors, all women and children, belonging to two families.

As I looked through my viewfinder, taking pictures, my body shook with emotion and anger. I fought to hold the camera steady. I saw that the children were trembling, too, out of fear. They looked at me and then gazed back at the shelter in disbelief. The women's faces were mud-smeared and blank. They appeared so dazed that they didn't seem to know if they were alive or dead. Somehow the pictures came out perfectly. The photographs are alive with meaning, even today, just like a living witness faithfully recounting the horror of what happened.

Quang Tri, 1972 Resting before the next fight, NVA soldiers read letters inside a bunker within the ancient citadel of Quang Tri, the first major city south of the DMZ. After capturing the city on May 1 during the Eastertide offensive, the North Vietnamese resisted a summer-long siege that would go down as one of the bloodiest battles of the war.

DOAN CONG TINH

OPPOSITE

Quang Tri, July 1972 Amid the remains of downtown Quang Tri, NVA officer Cao Xuan Khuong gets a haircut during a lull in the fighting. By the battle's end, on September 15, the entire city had been reduced to rubble. "Quang Tri was the deadliest ground," says the photographer, who documented the worst of the fighting.

DOAN CONG TINH

Southern Laos, 1972 NVA soldiers dash across open ground near strategic Highway 9 during Operation Lam Son 719, the South's failed attempt to cut the Ho Chi Minh Trail. Says the photographer, who was a veteran of the war against the French, "We were more alive in wartime, working in the border between life and death."

NGUYEN DINH UU

Quang Tri, 1972 NVA soldiers wander among the remains of the
former French governor's mansion after their capture of Quang Tri.
Composed of seven negatives, this panorama shows a row of elegant
French colonial mansions. None were left standing.

DOAN CONG TINH

OPPOSITE

Quang Tri, 1972 NVA troops storm the ruins of Quang Tri during the Eastertide offensive. Almost all U.S. ground forces had been withdrawn from the city, and the North timed the offensive to coincide with Richard Nixon's reelection campaign, knowing of his reluctance to recommit American troops as the U.S. was winding down its role in Vietnam.

LE MINH TRUONG

FOLLOWING PAGES

Quang Tri, 1970 NVA soldiers (left) rush through the citadel en route to capturing an ARVN position. By the end of 1970, America's "Vietnamization" program—the turning over of equipment and combat responsibilities to the South Vietnamese—was in full swing, and the ARVN was one of the largest and best equipped forces in the world.

DOAN CONG TINH

Quang Tri, 1972 NVA antiaircraft gunners (right) shoot at U.S. planes during the Eastertide offensive. White phosphorous flares drift down at upper left, combining with the flash from the gun to illuminate this nighttime scene. The American response to the North's capture of Quang Tri was the mining of Haiphong Harbor and intensified bombing.

LE MINH TRUONG

Quang Tri, 1970 An NVA artillery unit runs toward a new position during a B-52 raid. "To dislodge us," says the photographer, "the Americans used all kinds of bombs, even a kind that floated down on parachutes, one coming after another like beads on a rosary, and which on impact plowed up and destroyed our trenches and tunnels."

DOAN CONG TINH

Quang Tri, 1970 An NVA radio operator relays information during a battle in which the North Vietnamese fought against an armored unit of ARVN.

DOAN CONG TINH

Southern Laos, 1971 Armed with nothing more than a pistol, an NVA infantry officer rallies his men and leads the attack on an ARVN position on Hill 723 during Operation Lam Son 719. ARVN's foray into Laos was doomed from the start. Fielding only two divisions, they ran up against four seasoned NVA divisions that possessed superior artillery.

PHOTOGRAPHER UNKNOWN

Southern Laos, 1972 NVA soldiers plant their flag on an enemy firebase amid hastily made body bags and discarded weapons. The photographer recalls that moments such as this were fleeting: Once an ARVN base was overrun, U.S. bombers would arrive shortly thereafter to destroy it, denying the NVA the use of the fortification.
DOAN CONG TINH

OPPOSITE

Quang Tri, July 1972 Injured NVA soldier Luong Van Bao holds a live grenade as a medic tends to his wounds. Hit by shrapnel from offshore U.S. Navy artillery, Bao had to be restrained for treatment. All but three soldiers in his unit had been killed, and because their responsibility was to hold the front line, he wanted to run out at the enemy.

DOAN CONG TINH

Southern Laos, 1971 A dead ARVN soldier lies with his antitank weapon during Operation Lam Son 719. "Despite how well-equipped they were, they still suffered the same fate," says the photographer. Impeded by rugged terrain and denied U.S. air support because of unseasonably rainy weather, the South's best units suffered 50 percent casualties.

DOAN CONG TINH

Quang Tri, March 31, 1972 A wounded ARVN soldier grimaces in pain beside another prisoner at a firebase overrun by the NVA. The two soldiers were transferred to Hanoi and later released. "War is suffering," observes the photographer, "and this is what I wanted to show in this photograph. His face tells the story."

DOAN CONG TINH

Tay Nguyen, March 4, 1971 ARVN troops captured in Ngoc Ta Ba await their fate. Southern soldiers lacked the esprit de corps of their Northern counterparts. Forced into involuntary service of indefinite length, ARVN troops too often had to serve under officers who were appointed for their political connections and not their ability.

LUONG TAM

OPPOSITE

Tay Ninh, 1969 Dejected ARVN prisoners listen to a lecture on the policies of the NLF. Despite a lack of dedication to the war's purpose among many Southerners, some units fought bravely and well, among them the Airborne Division, 1st Infantry, and Marines. In all, ARVN forces suffered 243,000 dead and a half million seriously wounded.

HONG CHI

Southern Laos, April 1971

NVA soldiers smile for souvenir photos at Hill 456 during Operation Lam Son 719. The soldiers were killed shortly after these photos were made. The pictures later ran in the army paper, and the mother of one of the dead soldiers tried to contact the photographer, believing her son was still alive.

DOAN CONG TINH

BIRTH OF A NATION

CHAPTER FIVE

Final victory came in an unexpected rush. There had been a period of relative calm after the massive '72 campaign by the North had taken a chunk out of the top of the South. The peace talks in Paris had progressed to the point where the National Liberation Front was recognized, and joint talks about the future had moved to the U.S. military's Camp Davis next to the Saigon airport. This was meant to prepare the ground for POW exchanges, though in reality the negotiations were a means of tacitly endorsing the Viet Cong's right to govern already liberated territory. Another war would now ensue, a war of land grabs.

Next door, the "sideshow" in Cambodia was not characterized by the same gentlemanly approach. The Hanoi-sponsored Khmer Rouge, under Pol Pot, swept across the countryside, fitfully opposed by a demoralized, corrupt regime led by Lon Nol. There was virtually no U.S. ground presence to extract, the American role in Cambodia having been supply and massive aerial support. The Khmer Rouge, mostly civilians, suffered thousands of casualties. Collateral damage and friendly fire accounted for many more, forcing survivors to flee for urban cover. Despite North Vietnam's

Saigon, May 1, 1975
Amid the bedlam of liberation, NVA troops mingle with Saigon residents in front of the presidential palace the day after the war ended. When the tanks and soldiers first rolled into the city, people were too frightened to come out. South Vietnamese President Nguyen Van Thieu had abandoned the capital days earlier.
LAM HONG

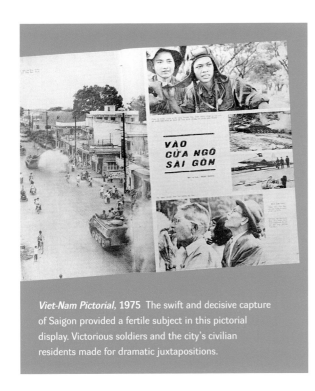

Viet-Nam Pictorial, **1975** The swift and decisive capture of Saigon provided a fertile subject in this pictorial display. Victorious soldiers and the city's civilian residents made for dramatic juxtapositions.

heavy involvement in Pol Pot's activities, there was little photographic coverage. Hanoi was already feeling disenchanted with Pot, its erstwhile protégé.

On January 27, 1973, at the Hotel Majestic in Paris, a peace agreement was officially signed. It had taken the horrendous Christmas bombings and the minings of Southern ports to bring the Democratic Vietnamese Republic to signature. On that same day, Lt. Col. William B. Nolde became one of the last official U.S. casualties. Many hundreds more would become unofficial casualties.

It was a false peace ushering in what some would say was a third war—a war of flag planting and territorial stakeouts. At Camp Davis the contesting parties haggled over POW releases, districts occupied and claimed, the status of the respective forces. Meanwhile, casualties mounted, and disputed areas and their populaces continued to be collateralized. On March 29, 1973, the last 2,500 U.S. personnel rotated out and 650 American POWs were returned. For America, their release was a mental formalizing of the end of the war. Now that the casualties were almost exclusively Indochinese, the heat could come off the U.S. government and the President. The vicious small battles, once guaranteed front-page space, were now relegated to the foreign section. Western media bureaus drew down their staffs. After the heavy actions of '72 and the POW exchanges, it was hard to drum up interest in the war.

Conversely, the coverage in Hanoi increased. Media groups and individual photographers could now roam the entire length of the land with much reduced danger. At several sites, their photos could be wired back to Hanoi, and irregular air links connected liberated zones to the North. Everyone became enthused by the knowledge that the last part of the slide was in place. Northern antiaircraft batteries, fed by convoys of trucks, now threatened the skies in the South; and the troop strength of the North's army had grown. It operated 12 air bases in the newly liberated areas; excess stores were stocked in the open, immune from aerial harassment.

The trail had become a two-lane, macadam highway for 240 miles north of the DMZ. Repairs went on round the clock, unimpeded. Newsmen working for the VNA could phone in their stories. With color film now liberated and shipped back to Hanoi for processing, *Viet-Nam Pictorial* was regularly running color features and covers, along with the traditional combat artists' watercolors. Dinh Ngoc Thong, one of Ho's "court" photographers, now shooting color, captured the last day of fighting on the outskirts of Saigon. He would keep shooting after the war, become editor of *Pictorial* and later chairman at VAPA. These days, he is retired, and his son carries on as photo editor and shooter for Vietnam's leading fashion magazine.

The period of the third war saw an upsurge in publications and films in the North. Sympathetic nations, along with Japanese and French publications, opened media offices in Hanoi. The North, the other side, now secure, merited the coverage it had never received.

Initially, the North was content to stockpile and creep forward slowly, creating discomfort in the once superior Southern forces. The latter were impeccably armed with all the latest military hardware, their troop strength at a million. The Northern force, waiting in the shadows, had created its own psychological advantage, as the greater percentage of the population in the South awaited its arrival with the hope of an imminent peace. Still, the Southern military would launch bloody spoiling operations, to off balance the next unremitting advance of the North.

The North was restrained, teasing time to verify whether or not the conditions negotiated would be observed. The POW/MIA case was the big stickler, tied as it was, carrot-like, to a 3.4-billion-dollar aid packet over five years. Not a cent has ever materialized or been paid.

After the 21st plenum of the central commit-  tee in the spring of the Year of the Tiger, 1974, the North's new watchwords were attack and counterattack. It had had enough of the Southern regime's prevarications and started to pick off strategic coastal towns; outposts were crushed in desperate fighting, with both sides suffering debilitating casualties. There was bloody fighting to the north and west of Saigon.

For the front's photographers it had become, as it had been for us, a matter of being in the wrong place at the right time—or was it vice versa? Getting about the shrinking southern republic was complicated by the increasingly regular roadblocks on all the arteries emanating from the capital.

The liberated zones stayed that way and started to rebuild. Individual photographers, like Khanh in Ca Mau, made the first moves to collate their comrades' works. With the new security, local presses printed newsletters and the first local papers. Material shot in the deepest South now filtered safely back to its parent, the VNA in Hanoi. New media blood picked up liberated photographic kit, and the shortages suffered for years abated. The losses to either side got only brief mention in the presses of both North and South. In the West, our media was preparing for the inevitable—in Hanoi that meant victory.

Tran Cu shot an image unimaginable early in the war, along the Truong Son trail in Dak Lak Province: Three portage elephants, flanked by a company of bo doi, make their way through the forest, their progress heralded by local ethnic people. The fear from above is gone, the roll for liberation is joyfully strong. There is a sense of everyone—men, women, and children—wanting to be in on that moment.

The photographers were getting their stuff to newspapers and magazines on a deadline basis now. The amount of traffic streaming down the trail and the transports rolling home again, unscathed, facilitated the kind of hitchhiking that we in the Western media had benefited from in the days when the massive American logistics support was still an ongoing thing, and we could grab a ride with a U.S. transport.

Showing the suffering and the victims of war had become our stock in trade, a need

Loc Ninh, 1973
An ARVN MP supervises a prisoner exchange along the Vietnam-Cambodia border a month after the Paris Peace Accords were signed. The black areas on the sides of the photo were caused by an incorrect lens shade. Blinded in one eye during 1968 Tet offensive, the photographer was no longer able to look through the camera properly.
LAM TAN TAI

to record the brutal reality, the punishing imagery that our editors and the world were gobbling up. The Vietnamese photographers stayed faithful to their own edicts, barely photographing the horror that had made us famous. They had to document, in the accepted way of a totalitarian socialist eye, their struggle and the solidarity of their people with a just cause. Luckily, there were enough artistic wild cards, freethinkers, and artists among them to bend that straight-line mindset. The realism in their imagery becomes surreal, the alien brought in and integrated with an almost Bauhaus formality. It has a certain Central European, even Swiss, structure. A style emerges still redolent of the old portraiture, but superimposed on landscape. One can almost sense a feeling of release, of being able to turn the camera to the horizontal and let the surroundings dictate the frame.

No one behind the Iron and Bamboo Curtains had thought to donate to the Vietnamese cause a box of Horizonts, the Russian-made version of the Widelux panoramic 35mm camera. Lack of gear had led the Vietnamese to incredible improvisations. Their improv on the panoramic vista was to click off a series of sequential frames, moving the camera, usually without benefit of a tripod, across the subject. A sweep of 180 degrees of devastation. The individual frames would then be pasted together before reproduction. It was not a technique easy in combat, lending itself as it did to aftermath visions. Here we have the B-52 strikes against Hanoi and Haiphong; the city frontages of Quang Tri and Hue; an etched, snaking trail through the devastated forests of the Truong Son; the U.S.-donated detritus after the French defeat at Dien Bien Phu dotted with the white blobs of resupply parachutes.

Nghia Dung was one of the photographers who used the panoramic technique, splicing together frames of overrun Southern positions in the campaign of '71 and '72: The awkward painted barrels of artillery batteries amid a sea of deserted matériel, shrapnel-slashed sandbagged revetments. Doan Cong Tinh's almost medieval frames show barbed wire and bodies posed in almost the same compositions that haunt the imagery of World War I.

The waste of battle changes little in interpretation, be it shot by capitalist or communist, mercenary or media personnel. The message it spells out is the same: the hopelessness of conflict, everyone involved a victim. The fine line between winners and losers blurs into suffering and survival. Photography successfully blocks out the cause and reveals the horror of result. For no war brings any joy until it is over, and amid the wreckage and graves it is hard to determine a true victor. It is easier to determine who the heroes were. In Vietnam, they are to be found mostly in the endless martyrs cemeteries that serve as the war memorials in virtually every town, village, and military engagement site.

The Vietnamese have always been diligent in honoring their heroes and martyrs, assuring a national, spiritual tranquility. The hero kings and queens, generals and individuals have their names enshrined on public places, in literature, and in endowments. Recently, the names of dead photographers have joined the heroes' ranks, appearing on renamed streets in Haiphong and Ho Chi Minh City. The photographers were hero artists, their role as fighters secondary. The survivors of that fraternity have been accorded medals, honors, and a status that bestowed access to certain privileges during the tough, post-war times.

Liberation had come with a rush, with far fewer casualties than anyone had expected. It was not to be the bloodied retreat of the armies of yesteryear. Yes, thousands in the South did pull back in waves from the advancing discipline of the Vietnamese Peoples Army. Well-briefed local cadres of the National Liberation Front paved the way. Thousands of milling, terrified folks from every stratum of society fled fates that had been falsely instilled in them. There would be no bloodbath. Hundreds would perish, there would be rearguard actions, hard-core units would make isolated last-ditch stands as at Xuan Loc north of Saigon. Still, nobody wanted to become the last casualty. The unknown of unification with its attendant austerity was preferable to death.

As the VPA pushed south at a speed the high command had trouble keeping up with, trapped remnants of the South's army and government packed onto overcrowded freighters and barges, hoping to attain the possible security of Saigon. Few made it, and the scenes of their lemming-like lunges appeared on Western front pages, our disgrace at abandoning them. After a few weeks, the Vietnam News Agency would pick up and print the same frames.

Most of the scenes of liberation show a sense of relief rather than fear of an impending terror campaign, as we might have predicted. The discipline of the lead troops was taut, abuse of the conquered minimal and humane. Pockets of resistance did not continue resisting for long, for now their reason for trying to defend themselves had flown to exile. National Liberation Front and Northern photographers could walk upright now, free to move as we had done on the streets of Saigon, our "hometown" no more. The first edict issued by the Northern liberators was a name change, to honor the ultimate Vietnamese hero—Bac Ho. Saigon became Ho Chi Minh City.

The T-54 busting down the palace gates in Saigon provided an occasion for the two sides of the media to meet and create almost identical iconic frames. The images of defeat were littered with the desolation of abandoned uniforms and equipment. But the rush to leave consumed the world press itself, and, because of that, the Western public would be spared the sight of suiciding ARVN officers.

When the bells of Saigon's cathedral finally pealed out in peace, they broadcast globally, tolling in a sad reflective time for all of us who had survived that long sad war.

Da Nang, March 29, 1975
An NVA tank enters Da Nang, the South's second largest city, where a million refugees had converged. Da Nang fell the next day, one month before the fall of Saigon. The North's final offensive accelerated as the NVA went farther south, with cities rapidly falling one after another, and ARVN units retreating toward Saigon.

VIET LONG

Hoa Binh, 1975 Heading jauntily toward victory, NVA recruits march through the mountainous region southwest of Hanoi on the way south. When the photographer took this image he was considered too old to go to the front lines. He was still able to contribute to the cause by creating inspirational scenes reminiscent of Soviet propaganda photographs.

NGUYEN DINH UU

Hanoi suburbs, 1973 Women perform a traditional Vietnamese dance for tank soldiers to celebrate the signing of the Paris peace agreement, which signaled the withdrawal of U.S. combat forces from the war. "The juxtaposition of lovely women with machines of war," observes the photographer, "was a combination the Vietnamese had grown accustomed to by this time."

DOAN CONG TINH

Loc Ninh, 1967 A Viet Cong guerrilla waits out the rain under a shelter on the Ho Chi Minh Trail along the Vietnam-Cambodia border. The trickle of trucks rolling by would grow to an armada by war's end, when the trail was able to accommodate more than a dozen divisions of NVA troops converging on the South for the final push toward Saigon.

PHAM KHAC

Vinh Phu Province, January 1, 1973

North Vietnamese pilots listen to orders at a remote air base only
days after the Christmas bombings, the intensive 11-day aerial assault
intended to prod the North into meaningful peace negotiations. The
Russian MIGs were kept safely inside a limestone cavern in the
mountains northwest of Hanoi.

DOAN CONG TINH

Hanoi, March 26, 1973

Following the signing of the Paris Peace Accords, North Vietnamese sailors celebrate victory at Hang Day Stadium on the anniversary of the founding of Communist Youth Day. Nearly five years in negotiation, the Peace Accords gave the U.S. "peace with honor" and permitted the removal of its last ground troops.

MAI NAM

Hanoi, October 1973

A military parade on the outskirts of Hanoi displays equipment earmarked for use in the war's final campaign, which was named for Ho Chi Minh. Such a gathering of military hardware only took place after the signing of the Paris Peace Accords, when the North knew that their equipment was safe from U.S. bombs.

DOAN CONG TINH

OPPOSITE

Hue, March 1975 Jagged relics of war litter the port in Hue, the old
imperial capital of Vietnam. The worth of U.S. matériel destroyed or
abandoned by ARVN troops amounted to millions of dollars. Hue fell on
March 26, four days before Da Nang. The photographer followed the entire
Ho Chi Minh campaign as the NVA rolled south from city to city.

LAM HONG PHONG

Da Nang, March 1975 Barefoot conquerors, Viet Cong and militia—some in
a large city for the first time ever—gather on a downtown street after the
liberation of Da Nang. During the American presence, Da Nang had been a
major military base and supply port. In the final hours before the city's fall,
desperate Southerners took to sea in anything that would float.

LAM HONG PHONG

Saigon, April 30, 1975 NVA troops run past American C-130
transport planes on the tarmac at Tan Son Nhut Air Base. Only hours
before, the air base and the U.S. Embassy had been the scenes of a
massive helicopter evacuation in which 7,100 U.S. and Vietnamese
military and civilian personnel were ferried to waiting U.S. ships.
DINH QUANG THANH

Saigon, April 30, 1975 Viet Cong guerrillas push bicycles laden with war matériel across a branch of the Saigon River on the final morning of the war. Northern forces had expected a long, tough battle for Saigon, but the Southern capital would be theirs the day after they reached its outskirts. Only a few ARVN units offered any resistance.

DUONG THANH PHONG

Outskirts of Saigon, April 30, 1975 Rolling relentlessly on, NVA infantry and tank units approach the Southern capital on Route 1. Panic-stricken residents of Saigon expected the city to be shelled, but the NVA held their fire. The U.S., resigned to the fall of the regime it had so long supported, made no last-ditch effort to intervene in the battle for Saigon.

THANH HAI

Outskirts of Saigon, April 30, 1975 Detritus of war, abandoned combat boots write the closing chapter on the once vaunted Army of the Republic of Vietnam. Hoping to hide their status, fleeing soldiers discarded their uniforms. "I took this photo from the back of a moving car," says the photographer. "I wanted the car to go as fast as it could to get into the center of Saigon. I was just happy."

DUONG THANH PHONG

OPPOSITE

Saigon, April 30, 1975 Residents jubilantly come out to greet North Vietnamese tanks entering Saigon, although the show of joy was a sham for some, intended to hide their involvement in the war. Many would be subjected to years of "reeducation" in camps set up to punish those with ties to the South Vietnamese military or government.

DINH QUANG THANH

Saigon, April 30, 1975 A liberation tank rolls through the Saigon suburbs toward the presidential palace. The Northern victors would rule the South with an iron fist in the years immediately after the war; however, the expected slaughter when they arrived in Saigon did not occur.

NGOC THONG

Saigon, April 30, 1975 North Vietnamese tanks take positions inside the grounds of the Presidential Palace. Col. Bui Tin, covering the campaign for the NVA newspaper, was the ranking officer during the capture of the palace. Addressing the nervous Southern delegation inside, he remarked, "You have nothing to fear. If you are patriots, consider this a moment of joy. The war for our country is over."

DINH QUANG THANH

POSTSCRIPT

Once you have covered a war, most other stories are anticlimax. Life in a combat zone sweeps the range of highs and lows. Surviving is the name of the game. Emotions are suppressed until a more convenient moment. Life in a war is very black and white, life and death. The shades, the hues in between blur, the pain is hard to remember. It is hard to shuck off that feeling, so eloquently spoken by Brando in *Apocalypse Now*. "I feel like the snail on the edge of a razor blade." No film, no movie can put the true feeling of fear and horror on the screen. The moment is gone, unfrozen with the next frame and the continuity. We photographers have the privilege and the perverse natures to penetrate the profane moments of mankind. It is our duty to project these, for all peoples to see, for our children to pass on to theirs, that we might learn not to indulge ourselves in more pointless violence to one another.

In the meantime, we just keep living. In Vietnam these recent times of change have proved hard. Most of the war's lens men are in the retirement age now, though for the most part still shooting, still processing and printing. Still purists. The subjects they shoot reflect the need for tranquility and beauty, the balming of disturbed psyches. Their images of young beauties and soft landscapes still echo their traditional work. The new photojournalism in Vietnam lacks an edge, appears causeless. Discontent is assuaged by commerciality. Innovation photographically has not kept apace of the times; being a freelance or self-employed shooter is a difficult proposition in a state that is only just opening the windows of change.

For me, going back to Indochina like a repeat offender, intertwining with the Vietnamese struggle to put history in its correct mental file cabinet, has opened up an emotional flap of understanding that neither I nor they could have achieved otherwise. Analyzing the images and the methods used to produce them has resolved, often in emotive outpourings, our hidden fears and foibles. Through their openness, my own fragility has been bared, though not without discomfort. The mutual privileges and honor we have felt and shared together have been like the opening of a lotus. Past differences are now a shared peace and a certain pride in the photographs.

The last image here says it all. Two old ladies, finally reunited, the gulf of time and duress bridged. This war, after all, was a tale less of liberation than it was of reunification.

South Vietnam, May 1975 Elders from North and South embrace, having lived to see Vietnam reunited and unoccupied by foreign powers. Some 160 Vietnamese photographers died during the wars against the French and the Americans. "The survivors are called witnesses of history," says Doan Cong Tinh. "I don't know if we ourselves are witnesses, but our photographs certainly are. They paid the price with blood."

VO ANH KHANH

INDEX

ACKNOWLEDGMENTS

I made my first trip to Hanoi with the dream of collecting these photographs into book form. Without the early encouragement and help of Mila Rosenthal, Pham Hoat, Lam Tan Tai, and Lac Moreau, I could never have even gotten started.

The vibrant community of ex-war photographers in Vietnam warmly embraced this project from the beginning, especially Mai Nam, Le Minh Truong, Dinh Dang Dinh, Doan Cong Tinh, Hoang Kim Dang, Vo Anh Khanh, Vu Ba, Nguyen Dinh Uu, Ngoc Thong, and filmmaker Pham Ngoc Quynh.

Both the Vietnam News Agency (VNA) and the Vietnam Artistic Photography Association extended their full cooperation and opened many doors for me, in particular Ha Mui, Nguyen Toan Phong, Nguyen Thi Tuyet Mai, Van Bao, Pham Quang Hien, Nguyen Duc Chinh, Ho Van Tay, Xuan Quang, Ngoc Can, Thanh Tu, Dao Duy Can, Pham Toan, Dinh Quang Thanh, and Le Phuc. Darkroom technicians Pham Cong Thuc, Nguyen Viet Hoa, Nguyen Viet Cuong, and Ho The Sang were always a pleasure to work with.

Photographer Trong Thanh survived five years on the Ho Chi Minh Trail during the war, and kindly shared his precious images and stories with me. Tragically he was killed in his Hanoi office in 2000.

Madam Kien and Linh Phuong generously gave me access to their late husband's archives, which greatly enriched this collection.

Generous donations from Robert Bingham, Eric Tunis, Bob Ellis, the Gerbode Foundation, Sam Haskins, Maryanna Haskins, Tom Robertson, Jody Jahn, Laura Niven, Janet Swords, Peter Swords, Samuel and Leila Hall, and Brad Niven made this project possible.

Bright-eyed translator Chau Doan was a huge help and a good friend. Thanks also to Seth Mydans, Richard Vogel, the Indochina Media Memorial Foundation (Bangkok), everyone at Laser Light Photographics (Aptos, CA), Photo Imex (Bangkok), Print Story (Bangkok), Phil Lippincott at Aztek Imaging, the alt-photo-process mailing list, Nic Dunlap, Tom Mc Carthy, Sara Colm, David Chandler, William Duiker, Carleton Swift, Jonathan Drake, Mark Gelinas, Chas Rubin, Niki Thongborisut, Andrew Todhunter, Dave Clark, Brian Bregar, Anya Schiffren, Bertrand de Hartingh, Bui Tin, Duong Trung Dung, Tran Luan Kim, Trinh Dinh Tien, Nguyen Thi Phung, Tini Tran, Martin Flitman, David Vanderveen. Thanks also to Tom Layton, Ron Moreau, Peter Maguire, and Samantha Marshall.

Special thanks to literary agent Carol Mann.

Thanks to photographers Philip Jones Griffiths, Greg Davis, Horst Faas, and Daniel Schwartz, who gave me encouragement and direction.

Mediterraneo restaurant (Hanoi), Au Lac Cafe (Hanoi), and Restaurant 13 (Saigon) kept our bellies happy. The staff and management at the Desyloia and Sunway hotels in Hanoi, and the Grand Hotel in Saigon made working in Vietnam a real pleasure.

Without the keen eye of book designer Bill Marr and the fine editorial team of Karen Kostyal, Becky Lescaze, Paul Martin, and Martina Nicolls, this book would never have come together so well.

Sound legal advice was provided by Doug Oldfield, Agnes Tabah, and Ken Bouy.

Carol Livingston supplied encouragement and friendship when they were most needed, thanks!

And my wife Saowalak "Pum" Niven hung with me to the very end.

Special thanks to Lisa Lytton for her patience, open mind, and unbending vision. You made all of this a lot of fun.
—Doug Niven

I would like to thank the following: Photo Archive Group; Michael Perkins; Jeff Apostolou; Bob Ellis; Joan Bernstein; Robert Bingham; the Lucius and Eva Eastman Fund; Don Riley; Robert and Danielle Levy; Michael Hess, formerly of the Saunders Group; Steve and Nancy Einhorn, Freestyle Sales (Los Angeles); Thai Airways International; Light Impressions; Ann Colburn; Tori Lyon; Yvonne Yang; Martin Flitman; Chaz Rubin; Charles Melcher; Pham Hoat; Ha Mui; Nguyen Toan Phong; Nguyen Thi Tuyet Mai; Lam Tan Tai; Pham Cong Thuc; Ho The Sang; Nguyen Viet Hoa; Bui Xan Hui; Tin Nghia; and Chuck Nyguen.

Deepest thanks goes to the photographers, both those whose work is represented herein as well as those whose photos are absent, but who had the courage to lift a camera during the War.
—Chris Riley

Another Vietnam: Pictures of the War from the Other Side
Tim Page, Edited by Doug Niven and Chris Riley
Foreword by Henry Allen

Published by the National Geographic Society
John M. Fahey, Jr., President and Chief Executive Officer
Gilbert M. Grosvenor, Chairman of the Board
Nina D. Hoffman, Executive Vice President

Prepared by the Book Division
Kevin Mulroy, Vice President and Editor-in-Chief
Charles Kogod, Illustrations Director
Marianne R. Koszorus, Design Director

Staff for this Book
Lisa Lytton, Editor
K. M. Kostyal, Text Editor
Rebecca Lescaze, Text Editor
Doug Niven, Illustrations Editor
Bill Marr, Art Director
Vu Thuy Hoang, Researcher
Carl Mehler, Director of Maps
Nicholas Rosenbach, Map Editor
The M Factory, Map Research and Production
Paul Martin, Picture Legends Writer
Alicia Moyer, Editorial Assistant
Gary Colbert, Production Director
Ric Wain, Production Project Manager

Manufacturing and Quality Control
George V. White, Director
John Dunn, Manager
Phillip L. Schlosser, Financial Analyst

CREDITS: Pages 12, 24, 38, 39, 49, 56, 58, 61, 77, 80, 81, 84, 86, 90-96, 98-99, 101, 106-107, 121, 123, 130-131, 134-135, 140-144, 164-165, 170-172, 176, 177, 194-195, 202, 207, 209, 211, 216-217, 222-224, 228-229: Photos courtesy of the Vietnam News Agency. Pages 14-21: Portraits by Chau Doan. Page 23: Photos courtesy of Bettmann/CORBIS. Pages 24-25: Timeline text courtesy of the Public Broadcasting Service (PBS), from the Battlefield Vietnam Web site (pbs.org/battlefieldvietnam). Pages 26, 28, 32, 46, 48, 50, 108, 110, 112, 152, 154, 208, 210: Photos courtesy Viet-Nam Pictorial magazine; copy work courtesy Tim Page. Pages 34-35, 42-43, 52-53, 74-75, 114-115, 126-127, 156-157, 178-179: Oral histories collected and translated by Ron and Lac Moreau.

Library of Congress Cataloging-in-Publication Data applied for.

One of the world's largest nonprofit scientific and educational organizations, the National Geographic Society was founded in 1888 "for the increase and diffusion of geographic knowledge." Fulfilling this mission, the Society educates and inspires millions every day through its magazines, books, television programs, videos, maps and atlases, research grants, the National Geographic Bee, teacher workshops, and innovative classroom materials. The Society is supported through membership dues, charitable gifts, and income from the sale of its educational products. This support is vital to National Geographic's mission to increase global understanding and promote conservation of our planet through exploration, research, and education.

For more information, please call 1-800-NGS LINE (647-5463) or write to the following address:
National Geographic Society
1145 17th Street N.W.
Washington, D.C. 20036-4688 U.S.A.

Visit the Society's Web site at www.nationalgeographic.com.

Witness the remarkable stories of Vietnamese war photographers on video and DVD. Call 1-800-627-5162 to order "Vietnam's Unseen War: Pictures from the Other Side."

The exhibition *Another Vietnam* will be shown at the International Center of Photography, New York, N.Y., January 11 through March 17, 2002. It will travel to Explorers Hall, National Geographic headquarters, Washington, D.C., in April 2002.